YOU WON'T
BELIEVE WHAT
YOU'RE ABOUT
TO READ ...

The COOLEST STUFF on EARTH

A CLOSER LOOK AT THE WEIRD, WILD, AND WONDERFUL

BRENDA SCOTT ROYCE

NATIONAL GEOGRAPHIC
KiDS

NATIONAL GEOGRAPHIC
WASHINGTON, D.C.

CONTENTS

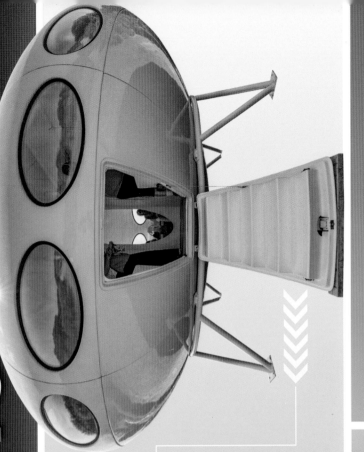

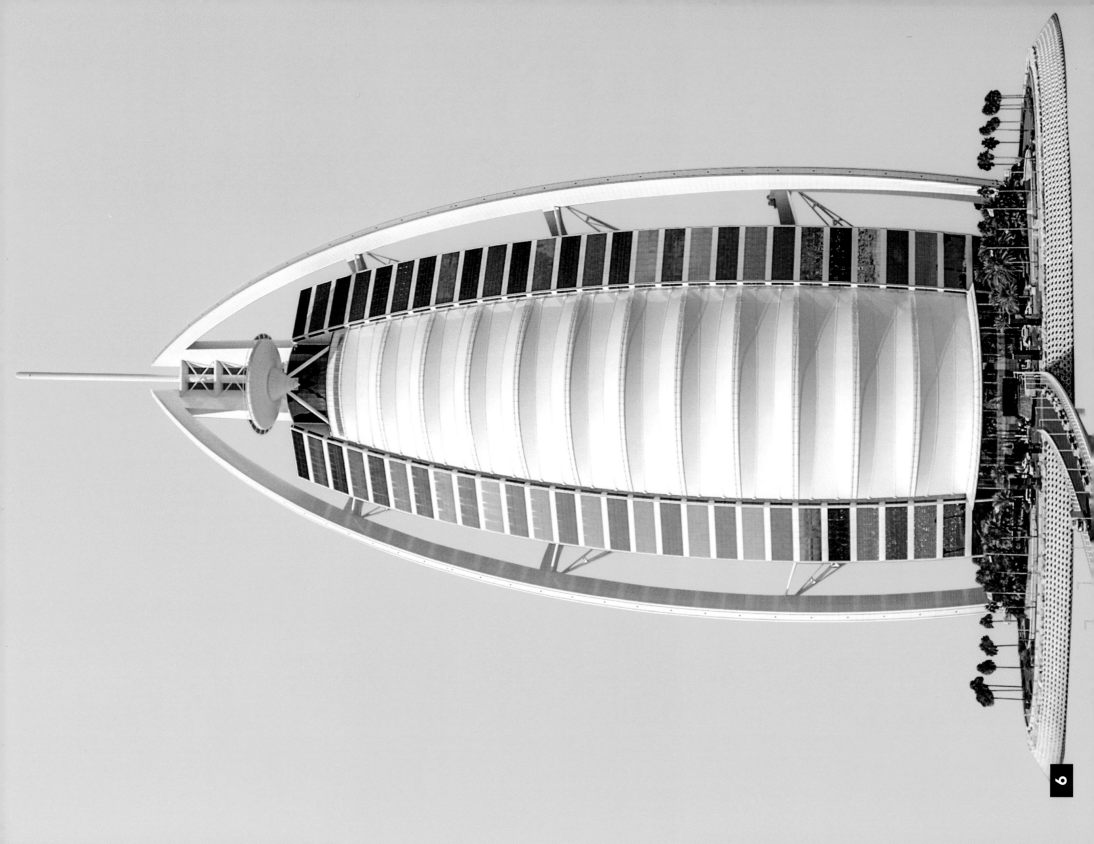

CHAPTER 1

MAGNIFICENT MARVELS

Sometimes the wildest wonders of our world are hidden in unexpected places, to be discovered when we dig deeper. Yet other amazing curiosities are right in front of our eyes! Whether these mysteries come from nature, are manufactured by humans, or are inspiring sites and accomplishments, this chapter is full of the most stupendous stuff we could find from around the world.

Sloth fur is home to HUNDREDS of INSECTS,

including sloth moths, which are found nowhere else on Earth!

WHY ARE SLOTHS COVERED IN BUGS?

A sloth's fur doesn't just protect its body, it's also an amazing ecosystem! This slow-moving animal hosts an abundance of houseguests on its body—including mites, beetles, and moths. Some of these stowaway species have evolved to live only on sloths, such as the sloth moth. What's the key to this odd relationship? Poop!

Sloth moth babies (called larvae) are coprophagous, which is what scientists call animals that eat poop. Adult female moths wait for the right moment to lay their eggs. When a sloth climbs down from its tree home for its weekly potty break, the moth deposits her eggs on the fresh feces. The larvae remain there, snacking away on poop, until they are fully grown. As adults, sloth moths feast on the algae that grow in sloth fur, so they fly into the trees to find a sloth of their own to call home—and the circle of life continues.

That's SUPER COOL!

AMAZING ARCHITECTURE

THERE'S MORE TO SOME BUILDINGS THAN FOUR WALLS AND A ROOF. AROUND THE WORLD, SOME IMAGINATIVE ARCHITECTS HAVE DRAWN OUTSIDE THE LINES WHEN CREATING THEIR DARING DESIGNS. READ ON TO DISCOVER THE STORIES BEHIND THESE STANDOUT STRUCTURES.

COOL LODGINGS

Chill out at Canada's Hôtel de Glace, a hotel made entirely of ice. Open to guests only during the coldest winter months, these chill digs have to be rebuilt every year. A team of sculptors and artists work for weeks constructing the icy inn. The layout changes each winter, but always includes a huge indoor slide and amazing ice sculptures. Each guest room has spectacular snow carvings, and some even feature fireplaces that are enclosed in glass—a precaution against them giving off too much heat and melting the rooms. Still too chilly? Guests are given super-insulated sleeping bags on top of comfy mattresses for frigid nights.

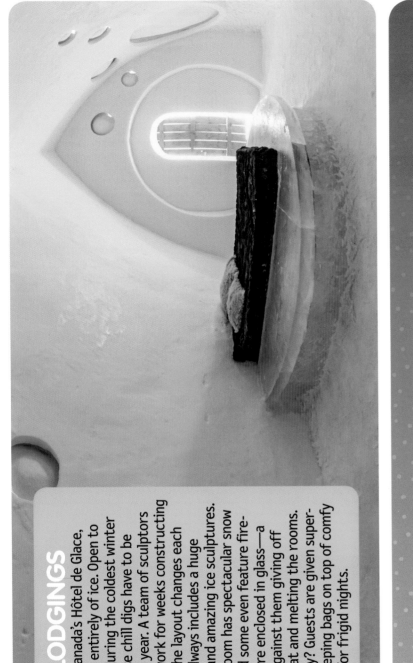

MIGHTY MOLECULE

Named one of the most bizarre buildings in Europe, the Atomium in Brussels, Belgium, is shaped like an iron atom—a great big one! Its nine apartment-size spheres are connected by a series of tubes and escalators. Built for the 1958 World's Fair, the Atomium wasn't meant to outlast the six-month exposition—but it has. Renovations from 2004 to 2006 replaced rusted-out aluminum with 50,000 pieces of gleaming stainless steel.

TOWERING TOY

Architect Sumet Jumsai had been struggling to come up with a bold idea for a bank headquarters in Bangkok, Thailand, for years. One morning, his son came into his office with a toy robot. Jumsai sketched a robot-shaped design and sent it to his bosses. To his surprise, they loved it. Finished in 1986, the Robot Building has won numerous awards for being a fun and functional example of modern architecture. The robot-like features all have a purpose. Executive suites are located behind the robot's eyes at the top of the building, and the communications antennae on the roof are also lightning rods.

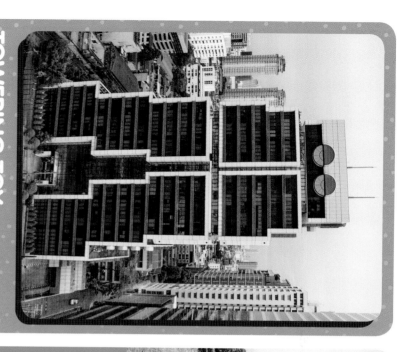

MOD POD

You don't have to wear a space suit to hang out in one of these homes. This round, squat building, known as a Futuro house, was designed as a ski chalet in the 1960s. An entrance hatch, legs that look like landing gear, and rounded windows make it look like a flying saucer. Its curved shape was designed to keep snow from settling on it, which would damage the structure. While new ones haven't been made in decades, several dozen Futuro houses can still be found around the world.

DANGLING HOTEL

If you want to live on the edge, stay in this lodge in Suffolk, Britain. One half of the Balancing Barn sits on a hill; the other juts over the hillside, appearing to dangle in midair. Why doesn't the building fall? The end sitting on land is anchored with concrete that's heavy enough to support the weight of the floating half. This type of building feature is called a cantilever.

SPACE-AGE STRUCTURE

No, aliens didn't crash-land in China. This building—headquarters for an online gaming company—was modeled after the U.S.S. Enterprise, a fictional spaceship from the Star Trek television series. The company's founder is a Star Trek super fan and hoped the design would inspire his staff. The sprawling structure is the size of about three soccer fields and cost about $100 million to build.

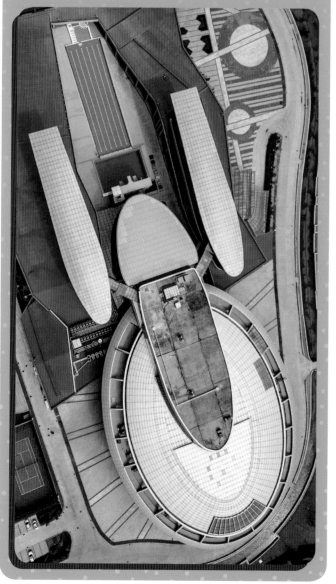

The world's

TALLEST

roller coaster

makes a **45-story**

DROP

...in less than
one minute!

THE KING OF COASTERS

Once riders are locked into their seats on the Kingda Ka roller coaster at Six Flags Great Adventure in Jackson, New Jersey, U.S.A., the coaster cars click-click-click slowly to the launch area. A horn sounds, and they're off! Kingda Ka speeds from 0 to 128 miles an hour (206 km/h) in 3.5 seconds. The coaster climbs to a height of 456 feet (139 m)—three times the height of the Statue of Liberty—before making the plunge down at a 90-degree angle, giving riders a sensation of free-falling. But that's not all. On the way down, there's a 270-degree twist that rotates the trains to dizzying effect. A second hill gives riders the sensation of floating.

How does the coaster make such a speedy shot to the top? It has a special launch system that uses a technology called hydraulics. This gives it the same speed going up that gravity gives it on the way down. The wild ride may be over in just 50.6 seconds, but it's an unforgettable stratospheric shot!

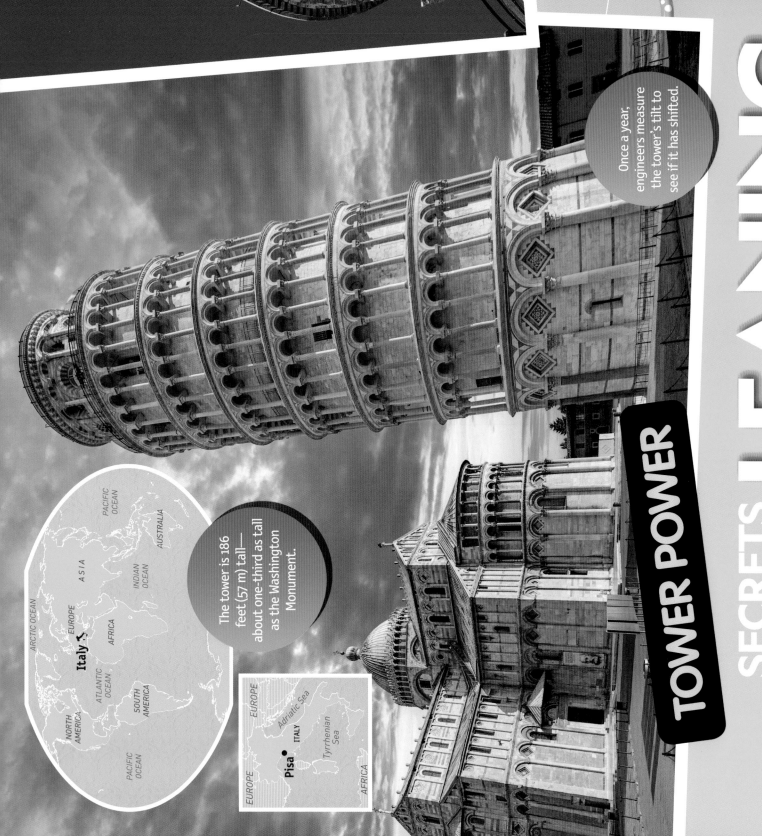

The tower is 186 feet (57 m) tall—about one-third as tall as the Washington Monument.

Once a year, engineers measure the tower's tilt to see if it has shifted.

TOWER POWER

SECRETS of the LEANING

One of the longest-running riddles in history may finally be solved. An earthquake ravaged the province of Pisa in central Italy in 1846, causing several buildings to collapse. But the famous Leaning Tower of Pisa was unharmed. To look at the tilting tower, you might think a strong gust of wind could tip it over. But it has survived several quakes in its more than 800-year history. Researchers now know why.

Lean Times

The Tower of Pisa is a bell tower, constructed to house the bells that call the town's people to prayer at the cathedral. The tower began to tilt while it was still being built in the late 1100s. The people of Pisa weren't surprised: Soil under the city—once the site of a giant swamp—is soft and spongy. One reason why the tower hasn't toppled is that it was constructed in many stages, with long breaks in between. In fact, after the initial phase of work, the Tower of Pisa began leaning to the north. Rather than start over, workers tried to correct the problem by slanting upper floors in the opposite direction. After the second phase of construction, around 1272, the tower slowly tilted south, the direction it tilts toward today. As a result of this back-and-forth work—literally—the finished tower has a slight curve in the middle, a bit like a banana.

TOWER OF PISA

Extreme Measures

Time and gravity took their toll on the tower, slowly making it slant even more. Numerous attempts to fix it over the centuries failed. A few even made the situation worse. In 1990, the Leaning Tower was closed for the first time in its history amid fears that it would topple. It remained off-limits for more than a decade, while engineers explored ways to stabilize the structure.

Suggestions ran from the serious to the silly, such as attaching helium balloons to the tower's top to help pull it up and straighten it. Since then, as the soil has settled beneath the tower, it has straightened about another 1.5 inches (4 cm). Due to its banana shape, it can never be completely straight. Nor would anyone want it to be. The tower's lean is part of its character and history—and a source of pride for Pisans.

leaned back to fill the gap. Declared safer than ever, the tower reopened in 2001, and its tilt had even been reduced by about 16 inches (40 cm).

Solving the Problem

Engineers ended up saving the structure—no balloons necessary. In a process called under-excavation, the team removed 70 tons (64 t) of soil from under the tower's north side. Gravity took over, and the tower

After 800 years of climbers ascending the tower's spiral staircase, the steps are worn down into wave-like shapes.

There are seven bells inside the tower, one for each note of a musical scale.

SURVIVAL SECRET

Italy is at a place on Earth where four tectonic plates come together. The plates are always bumping into one another, so Italy has averaged one earthquake every two years for as long as people have been keeping track of earthquakes. Why haven't these tremors toppled the tower? The secret lies in the soil. A team of engineers analyzed data from the tower's seismic sensors and studied the relationship between the building and the underlying soil. Their conclusion? The height and stiffness of the tower, combined with the softness of the soil, allow the tower to move with the vibrations. An engineer on the study, George Mylonakis, said, "Ironically, the very same soil that caused the leaning ... can be credited for helping it survive." Experts think it will still be standing—and leaning—many, many years from now.

FAKE Lake

When is a lake not a lake at all?

While this striking scene may look like a picture-perfect lake, it's actually an impressive optical illusion. Salar de Uyuni, located in the South American country of Bolivia, isn't a watery wonderland—instead, its flat surface is covered in salt.

PICTURE PERFECT

Most of the year, Salar is dry. The cracked crust forms tile-shaped patterns (like shingles on a roof) stretching to the horizon. During the rainy season, the region is sometimes covered with a thin layer of water. The slick surface acts like a massive mirror, reflecting the sky and creating otherworldly illusions. Wet or dry, it's a photographer's paradise!

HIGH AND DRY

Deep in Bolivia's Andes mountains, Salar de Uyuni sits atop a high plateau that's more than twice the size of the U.S. state of Rhode Island. It may be dry now, but 10,000 years ago the whole region was covered in water. The prehistoric lakes gradually evaporated, leaving behind a deep layer of salt. It's estimated that 10 billion tons (9 billion t) of salt cover the plateau today.

THINK PINK

This blinding white landscape turns a rosy pink every November, when flamingos arrive by the thousands! They flock to the flats to feast on fast-growing algae that accumulate in the shallow salty waters.

PASS THE SALT

Cone-shaped salt piles dot the flat surface. They were put there by *saleros*, salt harvesters, whose job is to gather and sell salt. Once it has been dried and processed, this salt could make its way to your dinner table.

A HAPPY HOME

Several species make this salty spot their home. Year-round residents include the rhea (a relative of the ostrich), Andean fox, vicuña (a relative of the llama), and viscacha—a rodent that looks like a rabbit.

NOW THAT'S FLAT!

Salar is Spanish for "to add salt," and this plateau lives up to its name. The shimmering surface looks like someone sprinkled the savory spice all over it! Rains dissolve the top layer of salt, making the Salar de Uyuni's surface smooth. Scientists have dubbed it the flattest place on Earth: With the exception of a few rocky "islands," there is less than 16 inches (40 cm) difference between its highest and lowest points. Because of its extreme flatness, NASA uses it to measure the distance between the surface of Earth and satellites in space.

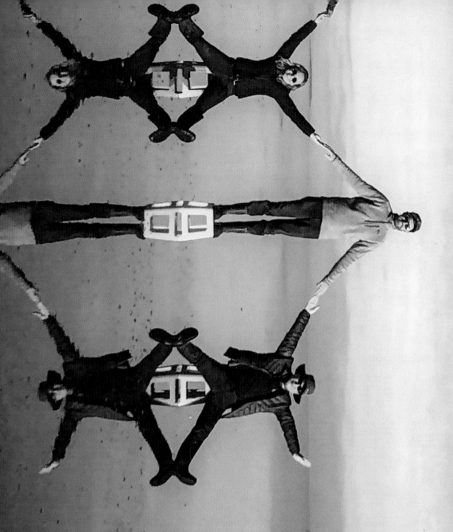

THE SECRETS OF STONEHENGE

People have long been trying to unlock the mysteries of Stonehenge. Who built it, how, and why? It was built about 5,000 years ago, before humans had a written language. So there's no record of how and why it was constructed. But since the site was discovered, people have had theories about Stonehenge's purpose. They range from burial ground (cremated human remains have been found at the site), to solar calendar, to temple for worship, and more. For decades, people have debated where these massive stones came from, how they were transported to the site thousands of years ago, and why to that particular place.

ROCK RIDDLES

Stonehenge is made of two types of stones—bluestones and sarsens. The bluestones each weigh 6,000 to 10,000 pounds (2,721 to 4,535 kg), about as much as two to three rhinoceroses. Their origins have been traced to Wales, which is more than 140 miles (225 km) away. The even larger sarsens each weigh 40,000 to 60,000 pounds (18,143 to 27,215 kg), as much as four to five elephants. These probably came from Marlborough Downs, about 20 miles (32 km) away, where sarsens are plentiful. But what if some of the stones were already there when the building began?

PITTS OF THE PAST

Archaeologist and journalist Mike Pitts has been fascinated with Stonehenge for decades. After leading an excavation there in the 1970s and then reviewing years of research, he theorized that two of the sarsens were already at Stonehenge millions of years ago, long before the first humans ever came along.

Under Pitts's leadership in 1979, a large pit was excavated near a sarsen called the Heelstone. Later, another huge hollow in the ground was discovered near Stone 16—the second important sarsen. Pitts believes these depressions near the two stones probably held the Heelstone and Stone 16. This finding suggests that these two stones are the very reason for the location of Stonehenge.

STANDING TALL

The Heelstone and Stone 16 stand out for a few reasons. Unlike the other sarsen stones, they haven't been carved or polished. This suggests they weren't shaped and smoothed by humans, as experts think the other stones were. Also, they align with the position of the sun during important astrological events in the Northern Hemisphere—sunrise at the summer solstice and sunset at the winter solstice. They could have been a kind of clock for early humans. Before there were calendars or watches or books to guide them, people could look to these stones for important information about their world and the passage of time. If this theory can be proved, it could be the key to why Stonehenge was built.

One mystery surrounding Stonehenge may have been solved. But many others remain, including how such massive monoliths were carried to the site and who the people were who built Stonehenge. What will archaeologists find next?

Heelstone

The Heelstone sits 250 feet (75 m) from the center of the circle. It weighs about 30 tons (27 t)—as much as five elephants!

The presence of two huge slabs of rock aligned with movements of the sun may be what attracted people to the location and caused it to become an important gathering place. About 1.5 million people visit the site each year.

Sarsens Circle

Stone 16

Bluestones (inner circle

Stonehenge is about 80 miles (129 km) southwest of London.

ATLANTIC OCEAN

IRELAND

Celtic Sea

Irish Sea

SCOTLAND

NORTHERN IRELAND

UNITED KINGDOM

WALES

ENGLAND

North Sea

London

★ Stonehenge

English Channel

FRANCE

United Kingdom

ATLANTIC OCEAN

AFRICA

EUROP

INSPIRED BY ANIMALS

SCIENTISTS TRYING TO SOLVE HUMAN PROBLEMS OFTEN LOOK TO PLANTS AND ANIMALS FOR INSPIRATION.
From household products to high-tech medical devices, nature has sparked many cool creations.

BOOM BREAKER

Bird-watching led to a big breakthrough. Railway engineer Eiji Nakatsu was trying to improve Japan's bullet train—one of the world's fastest locomotives. Sound, not speed, was the train's biggest problem. When the train passed through tunnels, it caused shock waves that created loud booms, disturbing people nearby. Nakatsu had admired how the kingfisher, a bird species common in Japan, can dive into water without making a splash—or a sound. Nakatsu had his team redesign the bullet train's nose to function like the bird's long, thick beak. The new streamlined shape made the bullet train quieter.

COWABUNGA, DUDE!

Beavers and surfers have some things in common. Beavers are excellent swimmers, and they jump in and out of the water frequently, like surfers do. They also have fur to keep them warm in cold water, while surfers wear wet suits to stay toasty. A wet suit works by trapping a thin layer of water between a swimmer's skin and the suit itself. Body heat warms this layer of water, creating an insulating effect. Beavers have two layers of fur: an outer layer that keeps out water and an inner layer that traps warm air next to the body and acts as insulation. Inspired by this dual insulation, engineers created a material that mimics a beaver's fur. The result is a suit made of furlike material molded from lightweight rubber.

PROTECTION DETECTION

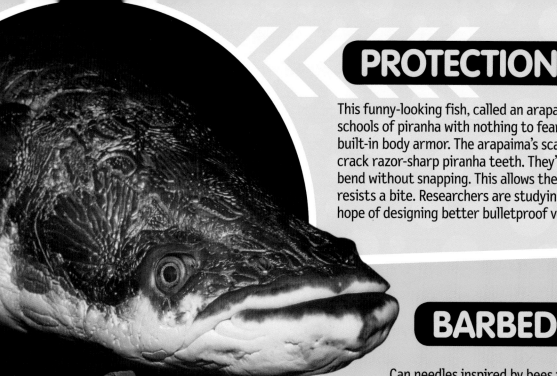

This funny-looking fish, called an arapaima, swims through schools of piranha with nothing to fear. That's because it has built-in body armor. The arapaima's scales are tough enough to crack razor-sharp piranha teeth. They're also flexible and can bend without snapping. This allows the fish to wriggle while it resists a bite. Researchers are studying arapaima scales in the hope of designing better bulletproof vests.

BARBED BUZZ

Can needles inspired by bees take the sting out of surgery? Doctors wanted better tools to use for surgery, so researchers observed insect behavior. Unlike straight, smooth surgical needles, honeybee stingers are barbed. These jagged edges help keep the stinger straight as it plunges into skin. In experiments, stinger-style needles had better accuracy than the old-fashioned smooth kind.

HAIR AWARE

It's no secret that cats lick themselves—*a lot*. Our feline friends spend up to one-quarter of their waking hours grooming their fur. All that time spent licking isn't the only reason cats are such great groomers. Scientists used high-speed film and special scanners to shed light on this behavior. It turns out that flexible, claw-shaped spines cover a cat's tongue, giving it a sandpapery feel. These spines rotate to untangle knots and release hair. Researchers want to copy cat tongue technology to make better hairbrushes for pets and people.

ASK AN EXPERT

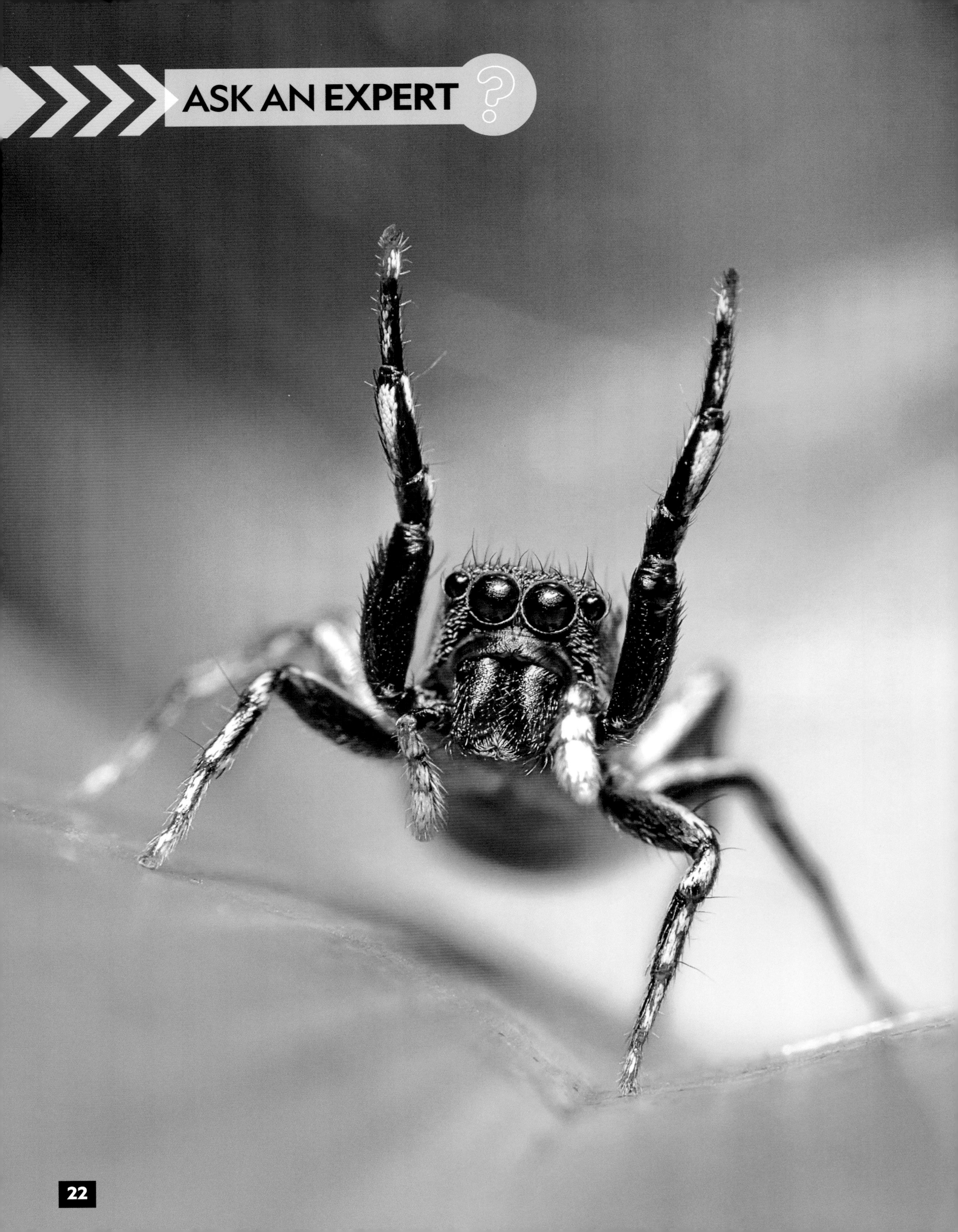

How do you work with bugs that appear on the big screen?

THE EXPERT: Steven Kutcher, an entomologist who has worked as a bug wrangler on dozens of films

Q: YOU'RE AN ENTOMOLOGIST, AND YOU'RE ALSO A BUG WRANGLER. WHAT DOES A BUG WRANGLER DO?

A: Wranglers are professionals who handle animals, and in my case, I provide insects and spiders for movies and get them to do what the director wants. I've learned how the animals work by observing them, and I work with their natural behaviors so they'll "act" for the camera. Being creative and solving problems are the best part of the job.

Q: IN *SPIDER-MAN* (2002), A REAL SPIDER CRAWLS ONTO THE ACTOR'S HAND AND BITES HIM. HOW DID YOU ACCOMPLISH THAT?

A: I was up on a ladder, about 12 feet (3.7 m) away, because I had to be out of range of the camera. I had the spider on the end of a paintbrush. I tapped the paintbrush, and that caused the spider to start to web down. Then I just aimed for actor Tobey Maguire's hand. He kept his hand still, and I aimed for it. It wasn't easy, but it worked perfectly. As for the actual bite, that was done using CGI (computer-generated imagery). Otherwise, Tobey's hand would have swelled up, and he wouldn't have been able to work on the movie for the rest of the day!

Q: SOME ANIMALS CAN BE TRAINED USING FOOD AND PRAISE AS REWARDS. CAN YOU TRAIN A SPIDER?

A: Training takes so long, and in the movie industry, they make so many changes. It's a lot easier to rely on their natural behavior and use things like light, air, texture, or temperature. For example, if a spider naturally moves toward the light, you move the light around so that the spider heads in that direction. If I wanted spiders to climb on a wall but not go to a particular place, I put wax on the wall. You won't see it on film, and spiders won't be able to get a grip so they won't go on that area. I try to get inside their heads. That's the joke I sometimes tell people—the reason I understand insects and spiders so well is that I have a really tiny brain!

Q: HOW DID YOU SELECT THE SPIDER FOR THAT SCENE? DID THEY HAVE TO "AUDITION"?

A: The director showed me a drawing of what he wanted, but there is no spider that looks like that. So we decided to paint it instead. I had to figure out a way to safely paint the spider, so I created a special harness to hold the spider in place and carefully placed it on the spider. The painter used a really tiny paintbrush and nontoxic acrylic paint. (Spiders have a waxy coat, and acrylic won't adhere to wax, so the paint peeled off in about 20 minutes.) And we did "audition" spiders! My assistant tried out the spiders and handed me the ones that webbed really well. I showed the spiders walking by tapping the brush.

The spider that bites Peter Parker in *Spider-Man* is a *Steatoda grossa*, a nonvenomous species also known as a false black widow.

Training spiders and insects is for professionals only! The American Humane Association monitors filming to make sure no animals (or spiders) are harmed on set.

23

CITIES OF THE FUTURE

As you leave school, your phone sends a message to a charging station nearby. It releases your e-bike and you hop on. As you zoom down the street, a sensor takes note and sends your location to a traffic monitoring device. Another sensor at your apartment building entrance lets you in, and the elevator is waiting to take you to the 19th floor, no button pushing required. It's 2050, and you live in a smart city of the future.

THE BIG CITY

When you think of a city, you might imagine enjoying magnificent museums or monuments, fantastic food, seeing a show starring your favorite singer, or having a picnic in a sprawling public park. You might also think about traffic snarls, loads of noise, and crazy crowds. Today, more than 50 percent of people on Earth live in a city, and that number is expected to rise. The greater New York City metropolitan area was the first megacity—an urban area with a population of more than 10 million people. Now there are 33 megacities, and that number gets larger all the time. With city skylines dotting our planet, city planners are getting smart about designing modern, accessible, sustainable, and tech-savvy urban environments.

A SMART START

In future cities, things we touch or pass may collect data through sensors. Using a digital network known as the Internet of Things (IoT), devices will interact, sensing and sharing the data with other connected machines. Objects we interact with in our homes and communities will be connected, too.

The IoT is already a part of daily life. Our phones connect us to friends and family, smart televisions give us access to all kinds of media, and digital assistants help us manage everyday tasks. And the IoT is already at work in cities. A sensor in a stuffed-full public trash bin in Boston, Massachusetts, U.S.A., photographs its contents and uploads the images to a department of sanitation computer. This signals a trash truck to add the bin to its route for pickup. Sensors of the future may guide delivery trucks, ensure the correct number of buses are on hand for a field trip, interact with sensors in drones, and share real-time data for safety and speed.

NURTURING NATURE

In the city of the future, sky gardens will be planted up the sides of high-rises. It will be easy to maintain these sprawling urban plantscapes because special sensors will tell where water and nutrients should flow—and open and close built-in shades so plants and trees get the right amount of sun. Fruits and vegetables will come from underground hydroponic farms that use water rather than soil and special grow lights in place of sunlight.

Water management is a key part of future planning, to protect wetlands and wildlife and to provide water for city residents. Heavy storms have become an increasing problem. Floodwaters need somewhere to go. Smart cities will have absorbent rain gardens called bioswales. Pools will collect and filter rainfall to provide water for drinking, bathing, and watering those beautiful sky gardens.

Sustainable technology will preserve our urban lifestyles into 2050 and beyond. That's a future to be excited about!

Conserve and Preserve
Undeveloped land will be set aside to protect our ecosystem and ensure healthy land, air, and water. It will also help maintain biodiversity of plant and animal species.

Sustainable Growth
Agricultural land will be located near small cities, reducing the need to transport food over long distances.

Urban Hubs
Communities built around urban centers will bring together residents, jobs, shops, and services. These urban hubs will be connected by mass transit, making travel times shorter and reducing the reliance on cars.

Experts project there will be more than 40 megacities by 2030, which means there will be about one new megacity a year.

Future cities will be powered by nature. Planners imagine outfitting new skyscrapers with solar windows and panels to harness the sun's energy. Some buildings might even have wind turbines installed on the roof!

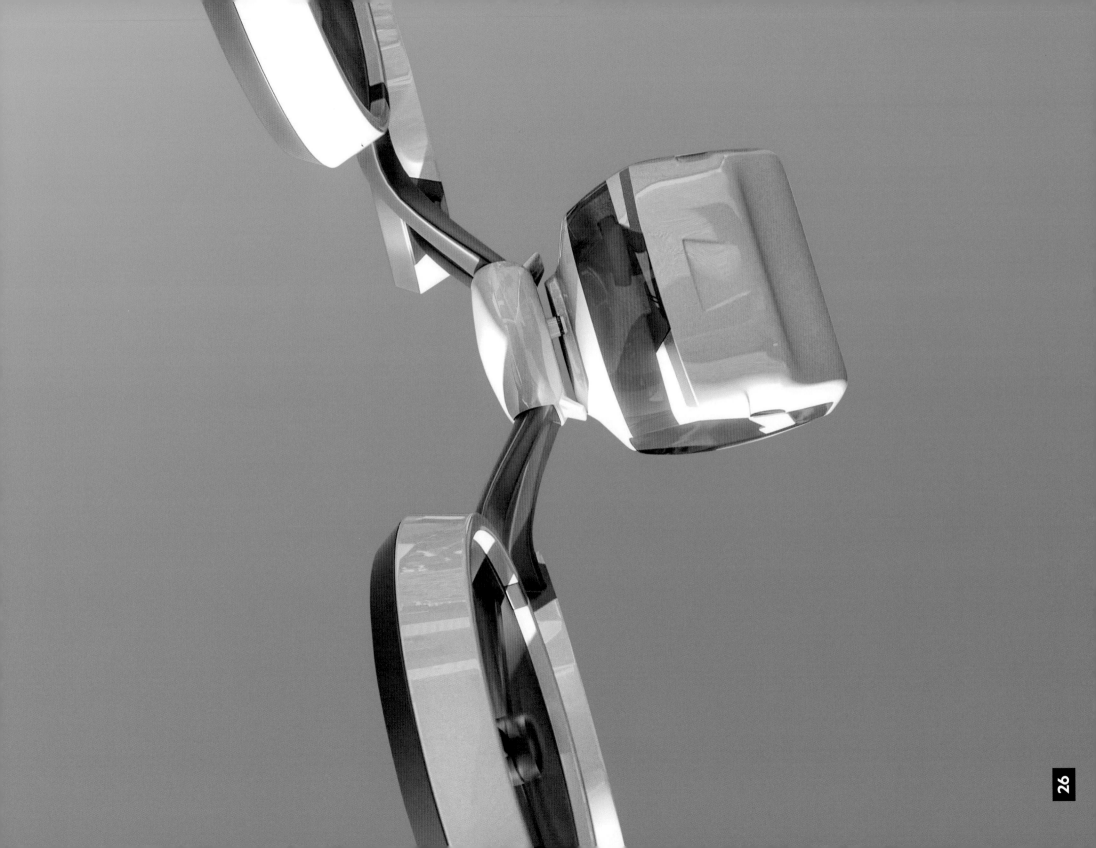

TRAVEL
UNRAVELED

Secrets lurk in every corner of the world, and this chapter is your passport to discovering them. Join a flock of mighty monarch butterflies on their massive migration, or hop from island to island to meet one-of-a-kind creatures. Blast off on a historic trip around the world, ascend majestic mountaintops, sail down the longest river on the planet, and jet off in a futuristic vehicle to explore dozens of destinations around the world. No matter how you get there, these pages may inspire you to wonder where you'll wander next!

BIZARRE ROADSIDE ATTRACTIONS

DOES CURIOSITY TAKE YOU OFF THE BEATEN PATH? IF SO, YOU KNOW THE WORLD IS FULL OF STRANGE SPECTACLES. WE'VE ROUNDED UP SIX OFF-THE-WALL EXHIBITS AND EYE-POPPING LANDMARKS YOU'VE GOT TO SEE TO BELIEVE.

LARRY THE LOBSTER

Tourists hoping to spot Larry the Lobster from their cars don't have to worry about missing him. After all, the 56-foot (17-m)-tall giant shellfish towers over passing vehicles. Larry the Lobster is one of Australia's Big Things—a series of giant tourist attractions along the country's roads. If you find yourself in Kingston SE, Australia, make sure to pull over and take a *shellfie!*

GIANT EYEBALL

You won't need to look hard to spot this giant eyeball on Main Street in Dallas, Texas, U.S.A. Made of steel and fiberglass, the artwork stands more than three stories tall. The artist modeled the sculpture after his own set of blue eyes. Is this a great attraction to see? The eyes have it!

HAMMER MUSEUM

One collector set out to celebrate hammers—and nailed it! This museum in Haines, Alaska, U.S.A., houses thousands of terrific tools. Some are just good for whacking nails, others are used by people with very specific skills, such as cheesemakers, bookbinders, and medical examiners. The hammers come from all over the world, but some were once used closer to home. One special example, a ceremonial pick used by a Tlingit warrior (a group indigenous to Alaska and the Pacific Northwest), was found when excavating the museum's basement. Visitors to Haines can't miss the place—it's got a huge hammer out front.

UNDERWATER MUSEUM

To get the best views of the art at Museo Subacuático de Arte (MUSA) in Cancún, Mexico, you'll need diving gear. Five hundred life-size sculptures make up this amazing undersea gallery designed to celebrate and conserve coral reefs. Coral grows on the statues, which then provide shelter for fish. Non-divers can explore the museum in a glass-bottom boat.

SULABH INTERNATIONAL MUSEUM OF TOILETS

Look, but please don't sit! From gold-plated commodes of Roman emperors to modern solar-powered toilets, this New Delhi, India, museum is flush with history. There are even displays of potty poetry and bathroom jokes. But the museum's purpose is serious: to promote better sanitation practices throughout the world.

INTERNATIONAL UFO MUSEUM AND RESEARCH CENTER

Did aliens ever land on Earth? This museum in Roswell, New Mexico, U.S.A., near a spot where some people claim a UFO crashed in 1947, encourages visitors to decide for themselves. Founded by two men who claim to have personal connections to the supposed crash, the museum also includes displays about other mysterious places and unexplained phenomena, such as crop circles, Area 51, alien abductions, and more. It's out of this world!

SOAR

up to 30 feet (9 m) through the air!

Draco lizards use "wings" to

That's SUPER COOL!

IS THIS REPTILE STRAIGHT OUT OF A FAIRY TALE?

The *Draco* lizard, also known as the common flying dragon, might sound like a fearsome fictional creature, but in reality, this reptile is only eight inches (20 cm) long from nose to tail. Found high in the treetops of Southeast Asia's rainforests, the flying dragon's small size makes it easy prey. So *Dracos* stick to the canopy and are always on the move. How do they travel from one tree to another without touching the ground? They spread their wings and fly! Well, sort of. *Dracos* technically don't fly, they glide. To activate their gliding gear, these lizards start by jumping off a tree limb. As they move through the air, they extend their long ribs out from their sides. This stretches out their skin flaps, which normally rest at their sides, and turns them into sails. These winglike sails catch the air and allow *Dracos* to glide from place to place. A second pair of smaller flaps on either side of their neck—along with a long, thin tail—helps them steer. These adaptations make *Draco* lizards tremendous tropical travelers.

SECRETS ⟩⟩⟩⟩⟩ of ISLAND

S et apart from the rest of the world, islands are unique places—home to animals found nowhere else on Earth. Whether tropical or temperate, polar or palm-treed, islands are distinctive destinations, and their strange creatures have intrigued people for centuries. Islands are incredibly isolated, so how did these odd animals reach them in the first place?

By Air and Sea

The Galápagos Islands, located about 600 miles (1,000 km) off the coast of Ecuador, were created millions of years ago by underwater volcanoes. Once just bare hunks of rock in the middle of the ocean, today this vibrant island chain is filled with strange and stunning species. There's the blue-footed booby, a bird with bright blue feet; the Galápagos giant tortoise, the biggest tortoise species on Earth and one of the longest-living vertebrates (the oldest known lived to be 152); and marine iguanas, the only ocean-swimming lizards on the planet.

Experts think the first wildlife to inhabit the Galápagos arrived by either air or sea. The birds and insects were probably helped along those long distances by strong winds that pushed them farther than they could have flown on their own. The islands' famous tortoises and iguanas likely floated over on rafts of sea vegetation or branches. Other animals, such as seals and sea lions, could have simply swum over. With no predators to gobble them up once they arrived, these animals thrived in their new home. After millions of years living on their own, some species evolved to become the unique animals we see on these islands today.

Floating Forests

While getting to an island by wind and water is common, one study of weevils living on La Palma in the Canary Islands (located off the northwest coast of Africa) shows another way animals arrive in style. Scientists found that some of the La Palma weevils were closely related to those on the neighboring island of Tenerife, about 82 miles (132 km) away. Most weevils on La

The Galápagos is a group of 127 islands, islets, and rocks. More than 25,000 people live on the four inhabited islands.

TRAVELERS

Animals sometimes "raft" on coconuts to cross expanses of water.

There are more than 70,000 different species of weevils in the world!

Palma don't live near the coast, so it's not as likely that they got swept out to sea on a branch or plant raft or floated away on the wind. Scientists think that instead the insects arrived on a floating forest, due to a mega-landslide that occurred more than 600,000 years ago. Landslides are common on volcanic islands, and researchers believe this particular event swept more than 50 square miles (130 sq km) of Tenerife into the sea, carried along by the ocean current, the debris ran straight into La Palma. Talk about making an entrance!

Alone Down Under

The island continent of Australia is famous for its unique animals, from

hopping kangaroos, cuddly koalas, and peculiar-looking platypuses to the tiny dinolike thorny devil, a lizard covered with spikes and bony plates. But these animals didn't travel to Australia—Australia took the animals on its trip.

At one time, Australia was part of a single enormous landmass. Over millions of years, that landmass broke up to form the continents we see today. As Australia drifted away from the other continents, a host of singular species travelled along with it. That's where Australia's remoteness comes into play. Out in the South Pacific with almost no neighbors, the unique species of Australia remained unique.

INVASIVE SPECIES

Some visitors to islands are not great houseguests. Animals and plants that enter an environment where they do not naturally occur are called invasive species, and some can cause great damage to native animals and plants. Sometimes these animals arrive by accident, while others, like mongooses, have been released onto an island to help control a problem. The mongooses were meant to control rats. But rats forage at night and mongooses hunt in the daytime, so instead of controlling the rat population, the mongooses threatened other daytime feeders, like geese.

Millions of **MONARCH BUTTERFLIES** migrate up to **3,000 miles** (4,828 km) every year.

It takes four or five generations to make the journey.

WHAT HAPPENS ON THIS MEGA MONARCH MIGRATION?

November means monarch madness in Michoacán, Mexico, when the region's fir trees are filled with millions of beautiful butterflies. These intrepid insects spend the winter there until spring, when they'll fly back north to Canada and the United States. But individual butterflies can't actually fly that far on the journey north: Monarchs make the 3,000-mile (4,828-km) journey north over the course of four or five generations. The first generation travels from Mexico to the southern United States, where it lays eggs on milkweed plants. Then brand-new butterflies make the next leg of the journey, and the process is repeated. On the way south, a single "super generation" of butterflies makes the trip. They fly on air currents that speed them along.

How does each new group of butterflies know where to go? Scientists have found that monarchs use the sun as a "compass." Changes in daylight hours signal that it's time to head south, while the sun's position keeps the butterflies on course. These insects also have an innate ability to follow Earth's magnetic field, which helps them stay on track on cloudy days.

Planets are always on the move, so the distance between Earth and Mars is constantly changing. The closest Earth has ever come to Mars was about 35 million miles (56 million km). A round-trip journey when the red planet is at its closest will take more than two years.

How will people travel to Mars?

THE EXPERT: Tiera Fletcher, structural engineer—an actual rocket scientist—working on NASA's Mars mission

Q: HOW CLOSE ARE WE TO SENDING HUMANS TO MARS?

A: Super close! We plan on having a human presence on the moon by 2024 and getting humans to Mars in the 2030s. But first we need to establish a permanent presence on the moon, so that we can test various new technologies and life-support systems.

Q: WHAT IS HAPPENING RIGHT NOW?

A: I'm working on the Space Launch System rocket, the largest and most powerful rocket that has ever been built. It will transport materials to the Lunar Gateway, a small spaceship that will orbit the moon—a pit stop on the way to Mars.

Q: SO THE MOON IS A STEPPING-STONE TO MARS?

A: Yes, exactly. Mars is millions and millions of miles away. It will take about seven months to get there, and then at least another year before the orbits align enough for astronauts to begin the long trip back home. We'll use our nearest neighbor—the moon— to run various simulations first.

Q: WHAT ARE SOME OF THE CHALLENGES?

A: The biggest challenge is what we call the human factor. How will the human body react to being in space for so long? To support human life, you must have a continuous supply of oxygen and water. On Mars, there's mostly carbon dioxide in the atmosphere. Where will the water come from? We'll need habitats that are already in place on Mars, so that people can stay there for a long time.

Q: ARE THERE SOLUTIONS IN THE WORKS?

A: Yes! A lot of different technologies are required for humans to travel to and sustain themselves on Mars. Some will allow us to replenish resources right there on the surface. One is called the MOXIE (Mars Oxygen In-Situ Resource Utilization Experiment), which can convert carbon dioxide into oxygen. We have the most brilliant minds coming together to create new technologies and find ways to optimize what we already have!

37

FANTASTIC FESTIVALS

EVERYONE LOVES A GOOD PARTY, AND FESTIVALS HAVE SPRUNG UP TO CELEBRATE NEARLY EVERY HOBBY, SPORT, FOOD, RELIGION, CULTURE, AND FORM OF ENTERTAINMENT. Check out some of these wacky gatherings from around the globe.

DUNG DEAL

At the Wisconsin State Cow Chip Throw and Festival in Prairie du Sac, the chips aren't for eating. Cow chips are dried pieces of cow dung, and they're used for chucking. How do you get the right kind of poo for the performance? Organizers carefully select the most promising droppings from grass-fed cattle. The chips are set out to dry in the sun and flipped like pancakes, until they form into fabulous flingers. Competition chips must measure at least six inches (15 cm) in diameter; if one breaks apart in midair, the fragment that makes it the farthest counts.

SWEET CELEBRATION

At the annual Cheung Chau Bun Festival in Hong Kong, thousands of local people and tourists spend days feasting on steamed buns, marching in parades, and enjoying musical performances. The main event is a competition to see who can grab the most and highest steamed buns from a 45-foot (14-m) tower. While the 100-year-old festival originally used actual steamed buns for this event, in recent years the towers have been adorned with plastic replicas. The winner of the bun tower climb receives a trophy and a year of good luck.

MUD MANIA! ▶▶▶

The region near Boryeong, South Korea, is very proud of its mud. The sticky stuff is said to be especially rich in minerals and is thought to have healing properties. To spread the word about this prized product, locals started a mud festival. People come to buy mud-based cosmetics and creams or to soak in mud-filled plastic pools. Others ride skis on mud, get a mud massage, or have their faces painted with colored mud. Ready to wash up? They even make mud soap!

KITE FLIGHT ▶▶▶

If you attend the International Kite Festival in Gujarat, India, be prepared to see some amazing airborne objects, from flying tigers and pandas to giant soccer balls, mermaids, and dragons. Thousands of kite makers and fliers come from all over the world every January to show off their skills in making and flying kites in competitions that extend over several days. All these kites in flight are an exciting sight!

RAVISHING RADISHES ▶▶▶

In mid-December in Oaxaca, Mexico, local farmers pick huge, specially grown, bright red radishes. Some can be up to 30 inches (80 cm) long. Then carvers sculpt the voluminous vegetables into works of art. On December 23, people come from all over to celebrate Noche de Rábanos, or Night of the Radishes, a tradition that is more than 100 years old. Judges choose the winning designs and award prizes, and visitors buy their favorite radishes to decorate their holiday tables.

Around the WORLD

Called circumnavigation, the long trip around the globe is no joke:

At the Equator, Earth's widest spot, our planet's circumference is 24,901 miles (40,075 km).

That's like running 950 marathons!

The first European expedition to complete the journey was led by explorer Ferdinand Magellan about 500 years ago.

BOLD EXPLORER

In 1519, Ferdinand Magellan set sail from Spain across the Atlantic Ocean with five ships, hoping to find a way to the Spice Islands (what is now Indonesia). The journey was perilous, and Magellan died before he could complete the trip. However, one of his ships, the *Victoria*, returned to Spain in 1522. After this long voyage, Europeans knew that a round-the-globe trip by sea was possible—and that the world was a very large place!

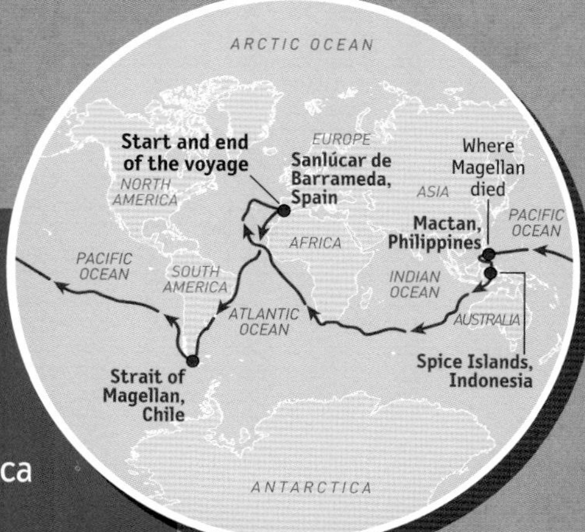

STRAIT AND NARROW

The key to success was discovering a narrow passage through what is now Chile in South America that connects the Atlantic and Pacific Oceans. Magellan succeeded in navigating through its rough waters, and it is now known as the Strait of Magellan.

ARCTIC OCEAN

Start and end of the voyage
Sanlúcar de Barrameda, Spain

Strait of Magellan, Chile

Where Magellan died

PACIFIC OCEAN

NORTH AMERICA

EUROPE

ASIA

AFRICA

SOUTH AMERICA

ATLANTIC OCEAN

INDIAN OCEAN

AUSTRALIA

PACIFIC OCEAN

ANTARCTICA

Mactan, Philippines

Spice Islands, Indonesia

DESIGNED FOR DISCOVERY

Magellan's ships were built for ocean travel. They were full-rigged, with three masts and large square sails. The sails pivoted on tall masts to capture wind from any direction, making the boats sleek and easy to navigate.

STAYING THE COURSE

In the 1500s, sailors didn't have GPS or satellite systems to guide their travels. They found their way with maps and compasses. A common tool for navigating by the stars and planets, and for calculating distances from the horizon line, was an astrolabe.

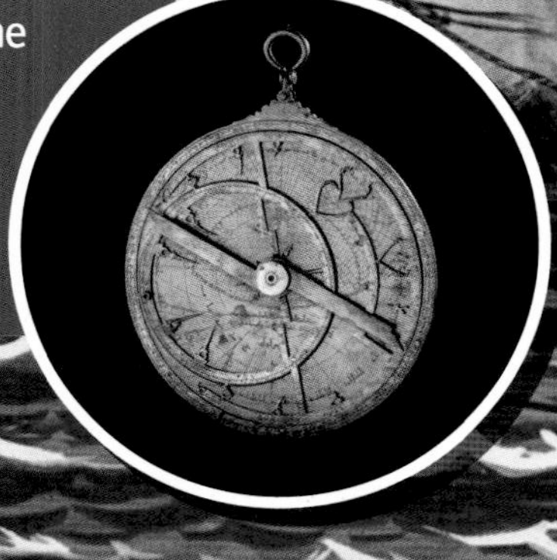

A RICH REWARD

When the *Victoria* returned to Spain, its cargo included cloves from the Spice Islands, more precious to Europeans than all five of the expedition's ships combined.

LIVELY SUPPLIES

Cargo on the ships included food such as preserved meat and dried fish, beans, cheese, and biscuits. Also on board were pigs and chickens, and dairy cows for milk!

AMAZING ANCIENT PLACES

A TRIP THROUGH TIME DOESN'T REQUIRE A MAGICAL MACHINE. THESE HISTORICAL PLACES HAVE STOOD THROUGH THE AGES AND OFFER SCIENTISTS, HISTORIANS, AND VISITORS A WINDOW INTO THE PAST AND A CHANCE TO UNCOVER SECRETS ABOUT HOW WE LIVED LONG AGO.

CITY IN THE SKY

Built at a height of nearly 1.5 miles (2.4 km), you might think this ancient Peruvian city is floating in the clouds, but Machu Picchu is actually perched on top of a mountain. Many visitors hike the entire 26-mile (42-km) Inca Trail to get a glimpse of it. Archaeologists believe it took thousands of workers to construct this mountaintop metropolis, built by the Inca nearly 600 years ago. After the Inca Empire fell in the mid-1500s, the abandoned city was gradually swallowed up by thick jungle vegetation. Archaeologists think the site might have been a royal retreat, and its amazingly preserved homes, temples, and other buildings show advanced engineering techniques.

CLIFF CLIMBERS

Canyon de Chelly in Arizona, U.S.A., has been home to indigenous people, including Navajo, Puebloans, and Hopi, for nearly 5,000 years. Homes built high up into the sheer sides of tall rock cliffs give clues to the lives of the earliest settlers. When returning home at the end of the day, cliff dwellers would climb steep ladders to enter their homes. Farming in Canyon de Chelly dates back about 2,000 years, and today, during the spring and summer months, some Navajo families travel back to their ancestral cliff homes to tend farms and continue their people's traditions.

MONUMENTS TO UNITY

Temples and churches are often built with rock, but the amazing worship sites at the Ellora Caves in India are literally *carved out of it*. Of the nearly 100 caves carved from the sixth to ninth centuries A.D., 34 are open to the public. Ellora represents a unique moment in ancient history when members of dozens of sects from three major religions showed tolerance and respect for one another. For centuries, Jain, Hindu, and Buddhist worshippers made pilgrimages to the caves. One cave served as a kind of hotel; there are rock ledges with beds and pillows carved from stone. Worshippers and tourists still travel to the caves today.

MADE BY MAGIC

The ancient city of Nan Madol was the headquarters of a dynasty of chiefs who ruled over the neighboring larger island of Pohnpei in what is now Micronesia—a group of islands in the middle of the Pacific Ocean, halfway between Hawaii, U.S.A., and the Philippines. To travel around Nan Madol and bring supplies—including fresh water and food—from Pohnpei, people cruised canals on rafts and small boats. The ruins of Nan Madol reveal an engineering feat of epic proportions: Buildings on more than 90 small islets were constructed from giant slabs of rock that weighed up to 50 tons (45 t). No one knows how the slabs got to Nan Madol when it was built around 800 years ago, but according to local legend, the stones were brought by magic.

HIDDEN HISTORY

In the heart of the West African country of Mali lies Timbuktu. For centuries, it was an important center of trade. Merchants brought goods from all over the region—including as far away as the Mediterranean—to exchange for gold. Timbuktu was also a center of learning. Scholars from around the world traveled there to learn from its vast libraries. But a series of conquests sent the city's treasure trove of more than a million books underground for safety. Only in recent years have these volumes begun to resurface. One find of 300,000 long-hidden books has helped historians know what life was like in 600-year-old Islamic societies and ancient African kingdoms.

Sensors, including radar, GPS, and LIDAR (a kind of remote sensing technology that uses lasers) will gather information to send to a car's computer.

Driverless cars will scan and communicate constantly with their environment, similar to how a virtual-reality video game gives a player an overlay of information on a scene.

GPS

LIDAR

Camera

Computer

Radar

FUTURE IN
THE FAST LANE

The idea of watching a movie, reading a book, or napping on a road trip isn't new—for those sitting in the back seat. But what about the driver behind the wheel? Driverless cars have been a part of science fiction nearly as long as there have been cars on the roads. But as computers and other tech become regular features in today's cars, companies are experimenting with robotic drivers, auto-drive features, and more. Is a self-driving car really going to be speeding into your garage any time soon?

HOW DOES IT WORK?

The key to most self-driving cars is the ability of a car to sense the world around it. Scanners and cameras using radar constantly search the car's environment and report back what they "see" to the computer. Onboard computers then gather all the data and tell the car's parts—mainly the engine, brakes, and steering wheel—what to do. If, for example, the radar spots a car in front slowing down, it instantly signals the brakes to slow the car's speed. Researchers believe that, in many cases, the computers and scanners can react more quickly than human drivers.

PRACTICE, PRACTICE, PRACTICE

The key to the cars' computer programming is artificial intelligence, or AI, which enables a computer to learn over time. Just as a human driver gets better with experience, the computer operating a car will add new information and driving techniques over time. AI will function

In machine learning, data and patterns help predict the likelihood of something happening.

like the brain of the car, processing data from the car's technology—such as GPS, cameras, and LIDAR (Light Detection and Ranging)—and taking in information from experiences to improve itself. As AI and smart-car technology improve, driverless cars will operate more safely.

WHAT'S NEXT?

Cars that don't give the human driver the chance to step in during an emergency are not yet allowed on most roads. But that may change in the future. Experts say that when all cars have this tech in them, they will communicate with one another to break up or avoid traffic jams, create smoother traffic flow, and prevent collisions. It's not just cars, either. This technology is being tested on boats, airplanes, and even submarines. And smart buses and shuttles are starting to hit the roads. How will a driverless bus know to stop to pick up a passenger? One day, there may be an app for that.

What's next? Transformers! Car manufacturers are working on cars that convert to cargo trucks, and vehicles with robotic legs that extend so they can climb over five-foot (1.5-m)-tall obstacles. That's amazing!

EXTRAORDINARY ANIMALS

All creatures—from the tiniest turtles to walloping whales and every animal in between—have an extraordinary side. Some might not seem like much, but if you look a little closer, you'll find out they can regrow arms, or see perfectly underwater, or even have glow-in-the-dark skin! All over the world, animals have adapted to survive and thrive in their unique environments. Jump into this chapter to be wowed by the secrets behind some seriously out-of-the-ordinary species.

Dogs can SHAKE

off a pound (.45 kg) of water in less than a second.

THIS SECRET IS ONLY SKIN DEEP!

The wet-dog shake may look silly, but it's more powerful than meets the eye. The secret is in the skin. A dog's skin is loosely attached to its body, which means it can whip back and forth quickly while twisting around. Scientists discovered a dog's soggy shake generates a tremendous force—up to 12 times Earth's gravity. That's more powerful than a race car speeding around a curve! All that tremendous force propels the water droplets off the dog's wet fur.

Lots of wild mammals use the same method our pet pooches do. Especially for animals that live in cold climates, staying dry is a matter of survival. The smaller the animal, the more quickly it needs to shake its skin to send water droplets flying. Water trapped in an animal's hair will lower its body temperature, requiring it to use extra energy to stay warm.

That's SUPER COOL!

SURPRISING ANIMAL ILLUSIONISTS

FORGET SIZE AND STRENGTH—IN THE ANIMAL KINGDOM, CLEVER QUICK-CHANGES MAY BE THE ULTIMATE KEY TO SURVIVAL. SEE WHAT SLICK TRICKS HELP THESE CREATURES TRANSFORM BEFORE THEIR PREY'S (OR ENEMY'S) EYES.

CLOAK OF INVISIBILITY

Want to look different in a snap? Try turning yourself inside out! That's how the vampire squid evades attackers. It lifts its eight webbed arms up and over the rest of its body, forming a shape that looks like Dracula's cape. This cloaklike posture protects the squid's head. And with its dark, spiky underside facing out, the squid is harder to see in the ocean depths and predators may swim right by.

FRILL THRILL

When a predator approaches a frilled lizard, it is treated to a fearsome display. At the first sign of trouble, this reptile from the dragon family unfurls long, colorful pleats of skin around its neck. This makes its head look huge—several times larger than it is. To complete its makeover, the lizard rises up on its hind legs, tail in the air. But it's all for show. As soon as the predator backs off or the lizard sees an escape route, it runs away!

SCARE TACTIC

Approach a hawk moth caterpillar, and you'd think you were staring at a short, chubby pit viper. Get closer, and it might even dart at you suddenly, just as a snake would. This caterpillar can change its look in a major way. It pulls in its head, puffs out its skin to make its body look larger, and repositions the spots on its back end to look like eyes and a viper's heat pits. It even takes on a snake-like S shape. Add in a scale-like skin pattern, and this snake look-alike can scare off jungle birds looking for a yummy meal.

HIDING IN PLAIN SIGHT

Transformation tactics are so crucial to the survival of the common scops owl that it can change its look in two opposite ways. If a minor threat comes too close, the scops puffs itself up to many times its size, spreading its wings wide to appear huge and threatening. But if something really big approaches, the scops will pull its wings, gray-and-white feathers, and even its face in tight. This makes it thin enough to look like a branch of the tree it's perched in.

COLORFUL COAT

Panther chameleons are quick-change artists. They have cells that contain tiny crystals to help them change color to show how they feel. The cells work like a prism or rainbow, reflecting light in different wavelengths or colors. If a chameleon is chilling out, the cells are relaxed and reflect short wavelength light like blue; but if it gets excited, the cells stretch apart and reflect longer light waves of yellow and orange. With a marvelous makeover, a chameleon can attract a mate, warn off a predator, or even hide in plain sight.

SECRETS of SHARKSKIN

Sharkskin may look smooth, but if you rub it the wrong way, it feels like sandpaper. That's because it's covered with tons of tiny toothlike scales called dermal denticles. (Dermal = "skin" and denticle = "small tooth.") Interlocking denticles act like a coat of armor, protecting sharks from larger predators. They also channel water, meaning the denticles direct liquid in the most efficient way possible over the skin's surface. This helps a shark propel swiftly and silently through the water. It's this fact that has fascinated scientists, shipbuilders, airplane manufacturers, and even swimsuit designers for decades.

Shark Superstars

Shortfin mako sharks are aggressive hunters that need to be faster than the food they're chasing. They hunt by swimming under prey and then shooting up to grab it. They can also shoot up out of the water, achieving dramatic heights of 20 feet (6 m). What makes makos the superstar swimmers of the sea? They have several advantages going for them. Their 12-foot (3.7-m)-long bodies have a sleek, torpedo-like shape that helps them speed along. And they are warm-blooded—their body temperature is higher than that of the surrounding water. This gives an extra boost of power and energy. But these are only part of the secret to their epic abilities.

When an object, such as a shark or an airplane, moves through a fluid like water or air, forces act on it. (A fluid is a substance that flows, so while air is a gas, it is also a fluid because it flows.) The force that pushes the shark or plane up is lift, the force that keeps it moving is thrust, and the force created by the water or air pushing against it in the opposite direction is drag. Mako shark denticles are a perfect shape for reducing drag and increasing lift, which is what makes an object move faster. And it's why the shortfin mako can swim a speedy 43 miles an hour (70 km/h).

Test Pilot Mako

In 2018, researchers set out to

examine mako sharkskin with a series of experiments. The denticles of this species have three raised ridges that point behind the shark. First, the researchers replicated mako skin using a high-powered microscanner, computer modeling, and a 3D printer. The artificial skin is realistic, down to its sandpapery feel. Then they printed it onto airfoils. Airfoils are the curved surfaces of a wing, tail, or rudder that aid with flight. The printed airfoils were submerged in tanks and measured as they moved in water. These tests showed that airfoils with mako-shaped denticles had reduced drag and increased lift, so they moved much faster.

Engineers may now have the knowledge they need to create faster, stronger airplanes.

Ship 'Em Off!

Barnacles are bad news for boats. These marine organisms cement themselves to a ship's hull, slowing it down and forcing it to burn more fuel. This hurts the environment and costs the shipping industry billions of dollars each year. Sharks—despite spending their entire lives underwater—don't get barnacles. Researchers at the University of Florida thought maybe the texture of shark-skin makes it hard for these hitchhikers to hang on. They designed a sharkskin-inspired coating for boat bottoms that shipbuilders use. Tests showed this innovation could prevent up to 85 percent of algae from settling on a ship's hull, and results are promising for banning barnacles, too!

Bye-Bye, Bacteria

A shark-inspired invention is taking a bite out of infection! Like barnacles, bacteria don't easily stick to sharkskin. University of Florida researchers brought barnacle research into the medical realm, developing a germ-deflecting material for use in surgical supplies and hospitals. Patterned after dermal denticles, it's even resistant to so-called superbugs—types of bacteria that can't be easily killed by the antibiotic medications we have now.

Maybe having sharkskin's structure gives almost anything superpowers!

Under a microscope, the tons of tiny teeth on sharkskin are revealed. Like baby teeth, denticles fall off and are replaced by slightly bigger ones as the shark grows.

When barnacles attach to ship hulls, they slow the vessels down. To solve this sticky issue, researchers turned to sharkskin for inspiration, developing a coating that will keep the hulls barnacle-free.

Dermal denticles are covered with enamel, the same coating found on human teeth.

Brown bears are famous for their long wintry naps. Before hibernating, these super sleepers eat as much as 90 pounds (41 kg) of food a day to store up extra body fat.

What happens when **animals** hibernate?

THE EXPERT: Dr. Frank van Breukelen, hibernation expert at the University of Nevada, Las Vegas, School of Life Sciences

Q WHAT IS HIBERNATION, AND IS IT THE SAME AS TORPOR?

A: Hibernation is a type of deep sleep during which an animal's metabolism slows for a period of time. While patterns vary, hibernation puts the brakes on several body processes. A hibernator's heart rate, breathing, and metabolism (converting food to energy) slow down, and its body temperature drops dramatically. Torpor is a state of inactivity in which the metabolism is lowered below the needs of normal activity. There's a range in terms of duration and other factors, and they can overlap. This makes it difficult to draw a dividing line between the two. Some people believe there's a difference between torpor and hibernation, but I see them as being on a spectrum.

Q WHY DO ANIMALS HIBERNATE?

A: Animals hibernate to deal with difficult aspects of their environment. Being able to hibernate allows an animal to withstand certain pressures. Predators are one pressure. I study tenrecs, which are really bizarre mammals from Madagascar. Snakes eat tenrecs left and right. So if a tenrec has already reproduced and is fat enough, it just hibernates! That way, it breaks up the predator relationship a little bit. Why be dinner, if you don't need to be?

Q DO ANIMALS HIBERNATE ONLY IN WINTER?

A: The word "hibernation" means "overwinter." We tend to think of it as a way for animals to deal with the cold and low food availability associated with winter. Ground squirrels hibernate to survive the low food availability of winter—but that's only part of the story. It turns out, if you really start looking at the evolution of hibernation, we think it actually evolved in the tropics! Much of where the tenrecs hibernate is hot and wet in the winter and hotter and wetter in the summer. So they may hibernate at temperatures above 25°C, which is in the low 80s F. They never see cold temperatures!

Q IS CLIMATE CHANGE AFFECTING HIBERNATION BEHAVIORS?

A: Yes, it is. Where it's not getting as cold in the winter, we see differences in snow availability. And that is limiting access to food. If you are changing food availability, you're changing the ability to hibernate.

Some birds, bats, and rodents like this dormouse go through short periods of inactivity called torpor.

This bizarre African mammal is not your average hibernator. Tenrecs are helping scientists discover the truth behind hibernation.

55

Superb **SEA OTTERS**

>> Cute, gentle balls of fur or rugged, resilient predators able to thrive in harsh environments?

Discover the *otterly* awesome features of these marvelous marine mammals.

HOLD YOUR NOSE

Sea otters don't need nose plugs to keep water out. They have special valves in their nose and ears that automatically close during a dive. This comes in handy on a long dive—sea otters can hold their breath for five minutes!

FEEDING FRENZY

Sea otters don't have stores of blubber or fat that they can turn into energy. So they must eat massive amounts of food—up to 25 percent of their body weight every day! Favorite snacks include crabs, clams, sea urchins, octopus, and fish.

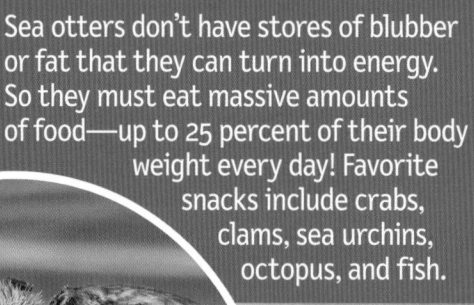

BUILT-IN POCKETS

Sea otters may not wear pants, but they do have pockets! Flaps of loose skin in their armpits form a kind of pouch perfect for carrying a rock to use later. This leaves an otter's paws free for hunting.

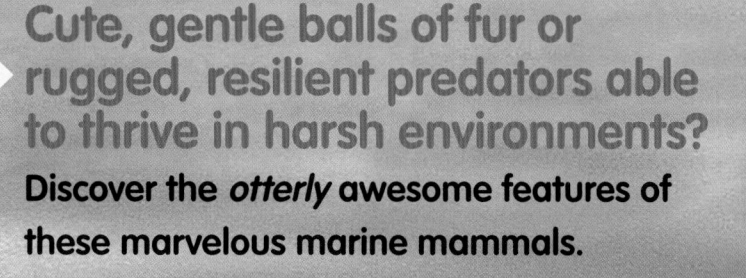

HANDS-ON HELP

Sea otters often hold paws while sleeping. This keeps them from drifting apart.

HAIRIEST ANIMAL

An otter can have as many as 800 million hairs on its body—roughly one million hairs per square inch (155,000 per sq cm) of skin! An outer layer keeps otters waterproof, and the inner layer of soft fur traps air to keep them warm and help them stay afloat.

TREMENDOUS TAIL

An otter's tail is about one-quarter the length of its body—and full of muscle. Floating on its back, a sea otter uses its tail to turn and steer through the water.

ROCK STARS

Just as people might use a fork or chopsticks to chow down, the sea otter uses rocks and stones to help it eat. One technique involves smashing shellfish against a rock balanced on the otter's stomach. Practice makes perfect: Pups as young as five weeks practice pounding their paws against their chest. By 10 weeks, they can pound while holding a rock and keep the same rock while learning to swim.

THE LOWDOWN ON A GIRAFFE'S LONG NECK

Why does the giraffe have the longest neck of any living species? One of the most iconic features in the animal kingdom, a giraffe's neck averages 6.5 feet (2 m)—about the average height of a professional basketball player! The most common explanation for the extraordinary appendage involves food: A long neck enables giraffes to eat leaves that are out of reach for most other animals on the African savanna. But experts now think this 200-year-old theory might just be a tall tale. New ideas are emerging, and scientists think that access to high leaves is probably an accidental benefit of having a long neck—not its cause.

OLD NOTIONS

The food theory was first proposed by a French biologist in 1809. He believed that by constantly reaching for the highest leaves, a giraffe's neck could stretch, and this feature could be passed down to future giraffe generations. However, this doesn't explain why other savanna animals, like antelope and zebras, didn't also develop long necks. Plus, a long neck has disadvantages, such as making it hard to hide and forcing a giraffe's heart to work extra hard to pump blood to its brain.

Famous naturalist Charles Darwin also linked the giraffe's neck length to its diet, but he had a different spin. Darwin argued that giraffe ancestors with shorter necks probably perished during times of drought. The tallest giraffes—those with the most dining options—survived to pass their long necks on to their babies. But there were still problems with

Darwin's position: Male giraffes are much taller than females and juveniles. If only males survived a drought by eating leaves high on trees, the entire species would face extinction.

POWER STRUGGLES

Another theory, which gained popularity in the 1990s, involves fighting. Giraffes might seem gentle, but males battle each other to determine who's boss. When giraffes spar for dominance, they swing their necks forcefully at each other, striking powerful blows with their heads and horns. Males with longer necks win more fights—and therefore father more babies. Yet this explanation doesn't explain why females—which don't spar in this way—also have long necks.

SPOTTING DANGER

If access to food didn't give rise to the giraffe's long neck, then what did? A 2016 study suggests that fear may be the real factor. The African savanna is a wide-open, flat grassland without a lot of hiding places. There are not many trees, and those that do thrive are spaced far apart and don't offer places to hide. A giraffe is like a living lookout tower, able to see enemies from far away. The ability to spot danger first is a big plus in terms of survival. While we don't know for sure, this simple explanation just may be a head above the rest.

Giraffe horns are called ossicones.

A giraffe has the same number of vertebrae in its neck as a human does: seven. But its neck is longer and more stretched out.

Vertebra

59

Dolphins have a **LANGUAGE** all their own—

they even call each other by name.

That's SUPER COOL!

WHAT ARE THEY SAYING?

From the moment they're born, dolphins squawk, whistle, click, and squeak. Using specialized devices to record sounds and capture data, scientists learned dolphins vocalize to communicate with one another. In other words, they speak!

Dolphins "talk" by using different whistles to say everything from basic facts to how they feel. Some species call to one another by name, using sounds called "signature" whistles. This is extremely rare in animals: Only humans and some parrot species are also known to have names for individuals. Where do these names come from? Scientists think that baby dolphins, or calves, come up with the names themselves. Researchers hope to learn even more about dolphin chatter by developing software to decode their vocalizations. Perhaps one day, humans and dolphins may be able to talk through tech.

SURVIVAL STRATEGIES

CLAWS, FANGS, AND TUSKS ARE EASY TO SPOT, BUT SOME SNEAKY SPECIES KEEP THEIR COOLEST FEATURES UNDER WRAPS.
Read on to discover special body parts that help certain creatures survive—and thrive!

LETHAL LORIS

Slow lorises look cute, but this species from Southeast Asia has a sinister side: It's venomous! Venom—poison injected through a bite or sting—is common in reptiles and insects but rare in mammals. In fact, the loris is the only venomous primate. Lorises lick a special gland on their inner arms that secretes venom. Mixed with their saliva, it becomes a toxic concoction that lorises deliver to predators with needlelike teeth. Lorises spread the deadly venom onto their own fur, too, to warn off predators. A loris mom may also lick her infant's fur as a smelly protective coating, then park the baby in a tree while she goes off to forage for food. Poison is a built-in babysitter.

REAR ATTACK

Bombardier beetles have a special—and sizzling—way of scaring off potential predators. A toad, for instance, that swallows a bombardier beetle will be in for the shock of its life. This snack fights back by blasting a jet of hot chemicals from its backside. The explosive gas-pass can reach temperatures of up to 100°F (38°C) and cause the toad to vomit up its last meal. But better late than never: Barfed-up bombardier beetles have a more than 40 percent chance of surviving the attack.

SPEAR RIBS

The Iberian ribbed newt has a secret trick hidden under its skin—it can stick its ribs through its body like spears! It accomplishes this frightful feat by flipping its ribcage sideways about 50 degrees, which stretches the skin to the point where it's easily punctured. A predator that takes on this animal is in for a spiky surprise. When the danger is over, the newt's ribs return to their original position and the puncture wounds begin to heal.

DECEPTIVE DARTER

The goblin shark may not be the fastest shark in the sea, but what it lacks in speed it makes up for in deadly dental deception. The goblin shark's jaw is attached to its snout with springy ligaments. When a tasty treat swims nearby, the shark can stretch out skin flaps containing a mouth full of jagged, razor-sharp teeth. Snap! An unsuspecting squid or other tasty bite is down the hatch before it even senses the shark is close.

STINK BIRD

For the hoatzin, the best defense may be a good offense—an offensive odor, that is. This tropical bird reeks of cow manure! Bad hygiene isn't to blame; its stench is a side effect of its leaf-based diet. Leaves are low in calories, so a hoatzin needs to eat a lot of them. But the bird doesn't have enzymes to break down the leaves. Instead, it has a multichambered digestive system that uses bacteria to break down plants and extract energy. This process is called fermentation, and it takes more than three days for the bird to digest a meal. That's a long time to smell so foul! Scientists think its stink may keep other animals away and help it survive.

Measuring from tip to tip, the wingspan of a snowy owl is 57 inches (145 cm).

SECRETS of OWL FLIGHT

Snowy owls soared to fame thanks to the Harry Potter books and movies. Like other pets in the wizarding world, Harry's Hedwig has magical traits. But the snowy owl's most extraordinary power—silent flight—is far from fictional.

Weighing up to 6.5 pounds (3 kg), the snowy is the heaviest owl in North America. Yet it soundlessly swoops down on the rodents it preys on, catching them completely off guard. How? The secret lies in its specialized feathers.

Fascinating Feathers

Scientists have been studying owl feathers for more than 100 years to figure out the secret of owls' silent flight. In 1904, a German zoologist studied flight feathers on several kinds of birds, including snowy, eagle, barn, and horned owls, and found that the leading (forward-facing) edge of owls' flight feathers are serrated like a comb. Other types of birds don't have this feature. In the 1930s, a pilot and avid bird-watcher discovered more features of owl feathers that contribute to silent flight: a flexible fringe on the trailing edge that reduces turbulence (fast-moving, noisy air), and a soft, velvety surface that absorbs sound. In a recent experiment, even the most sensitive microphones failed to pick up the sound

of an owl in flight. How is this possible? An owl's fancy feathers are just one of this raptor's stealthy characteristics.

Great Gliders

An owl's wings are large compared to its body—much larger than those on most birds of similar body size. This means owls can glide on air currents for long distances before they need to flap their wings again to stay up. Frequent flappers like pigeons and peregrine falcons create lots of turbulence, which means lots of noise.

Why Stay Quiet?

Scientists think silent flight helps hungry owls hunt in two ways. If

64

unsuspecting small mammals, such as mice and rabbits, can't hear the approach of a flying hunter, they won't scurry away before they can be snatched from the forest floor. Among owls, the ones that hunt at night are the most silent fliers. Plus, when searching for tasty treats in the dark, an owl must use its hearing to find dinner. Noisy flapping would interfere with the owl's own ability to pick up sounds around it.

Mute Machines

To create quieter airplanes, engineers are taking cues from owls. With more than 50,000 flights crisscrossing the United States every day, aircraft noise is a huge concern. Noise pollution isn't just annoying—it's been linked to human health problems and affects animal behaviors and habitats, too.

In 2016, a group of researchers designed an owl-inspired 3D-printed wing attachment that reduces aircraft noise by 10 decibels. That makes takeoff and landing about 10 percent quieter. Engineers are also turning to owls for inspiration in creating ultraquiet drones and other airborne devices.

Train Trouble

Airplanes aren't the only transportation that makes noise. Superfast bullet trains are world-famous for transforming travel. But these trains sometimes speed through busy neighborhoods, so engineers needed a way to make them quieter. Bullet trains get electricity through overhead wires linked to each train through a frame called a pantograph. Most of the noise the train makes comes from air passing over this frame. By observing the silent flight of owls, engineers designed the Shinkansen, Japan's most famous high-speed train, to have serrated edges on its pantograph. The edges break up the air so it makes less noise, just like the edges of owl feathers do.

As we continue to learn more about the mysteries of these amazing birds, who knows what other innovations owls will inspire?

The ends of horned owl feathers have sharp comb-like serrations that can be seen when magnified for a close-up look.

Great horned owls learn to fly when they are six weeks old.

NOT SO QUIET

Not all owls have the gift of silence. Owls that hunt fish for their main food, such as the tawny fish owl, don't have soft feathers with serrated edges. Neither do insect-eating owls like the screech owl (above). What do fish and insects have in common? For one thing, they don't have keen hearing, so owls that hunt them don't need a silent approach.

Surprising SNAKES

>> Fearsome and awe-inspiring, snakes are spectacular specimens.

Scientists have yet to uncover all the sssecrets of the 3,500 snake species on Earth, but what we do know is pretty amazing. Read on to discover some sssseriously surprising stuff about these superb serpents.

THE SKIN THEY'RE IN

A snake sheds its entire skin—or molts—several times a year. First, oil forms between the old skin and new skin layers. Then the snake rubs against a rough surface, such as a rock, to peel back the skin around its head. After a week or two of this moving around, the old skin slips off.

LASH DEFENSES

Eyelash vipers are at home in the tropical climate of Central and South America's jungles. Heat pits—holes under the eyes—have a membrane inside that senses heat from live prey just over three feet (1 m) away. These snakes are named for the bristly projections above their eyes that look like brows or lashes. Some experts think their "eyelashes" protect the snakes' eyes.

MAIN SQUEEZE

Boas, like this emerald tree boa, are constrictors. A constrictor wraps its body around its prey and squeezes. Scientists once thought that the boas were squeezing to prevent the prey from breathing, but recent studies suggest they're actually stopping the prey's blood flow.

python, are the longest in the world. This length helps them constrict the bodies of huge animals, which they swallow whole by opening their uniquely built jaws. Their jaws have multiple hinges and springy elastic ligaments to open wide enough to swallow birds, lizards, and even antelope!

SMOOTH MOVES

No legs? No problem! The most common way snakes move is by slithering. They move their bodies back and forth in an S-shaped pattern and use muscles to push sections of their long, flexible bodies ahead. Large scales on their bellies act like grippers to pull them forward.

FANGS A LOT

While most snakes have teeth, only venomous snakes have fangs. These long, strong teeth can inject venom during a bite. In some snakes, fangs are folded back against the roof of the mouth until needed. In others, fangs are fixed in place and always ready.

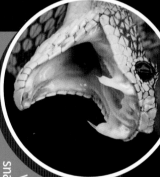

BUILT-IN HOODIE

This snake is the king of confrontation. When threatened, the king cobra raises its head high and rotates its ribs outward to appear larger. This hood isn't just for show, though. The king is a powerful predator that can strike targets faster than it takes a person to blink. Its venom is so toxic that a single bite can bring down an elephant.

CHAPTER 4

HISTORY'S MYSTERIES

Giant ground sloths forage for ancient avocados. Nineteenth-century farmers herd sheep on stilts. The world before you were born was a wondrous and wacky place! Today, scientists and researchers are working hard to piece together clues left behind by the people and creatures that roamed long ago, sometimes getting a boost from cutting-edge technology. Get ready to travel back in time to get a close-up look at astonishing ancient animals, amazing discoveries about long-lost civilizations, and terrific trends from times gone by.

Roman statues had interchangeable parts.

The **HEADS** were swapped out when a new ruler was crowned.

NOGGIN OPTIONS

If you happen to be at an art museum admiring some Roman statues, you might notice that something is often missing: the statues' heads! It took (and still takes) sculptors many days to chisel through expensive marble to create life-size works of art. Ancient Roman sculptors used a supersmart and time-saving tactic: By making their statues with generic bodies and interchangeable heads, they could simply swap in a different topper when a new ruler or official assumed power. The bodies usually included a flowing robe ending above sandaled feet, which was the wardrobe typical of the Roman elite, and then the sculptors focused their artistry on creating distinct faces on the heads. This was so much easier than starting a whole new statue from scratch! A new head was affixed with a mixture of marble dust and glue, which made the neck area weaker than the rest of the statue. Over the years, heads would often fall or break off, which is one reason why we're left with so many headless statues today.

That's SUPER
COOL!

The Angkor Wat complex took the work of 300,000 people and 6,000 elephants to build. At its peak, it had a population of 750,000.

SECRETS of ANGKOR

n the midst of Cambodia's steamy jungle looms a majestic medieval temple. Called Angkor Wat, the nearly 900-year-old structure was built in the capital of the Khmer Empire, a powerful civilization in Southeast Asia. Now the site receives more than two million visitors a year. But until recently, few were aware of something tucked in the forest beyond the temple—a hidden city.

Missing Metropolis

The Khmer Empire thrived between the 9th and 15th centuries. Many people worshipped at the temple of Angkor Wat in the capital city of Angkor, which covered about as much area as Denver, Colorado, U.S.A. Scientists believe that in the

14th and 15th centuries, droughts and other extreme natural disasters caused many people to abandon the region and move south. Eventually, thick forests grew over much of the area.

Built in the 12th century to honor a god, Angkor Wat was in continual use even after the capital city was abandoned. When a French explorer came across the temple in the 1800s, he spread word of its beauty, drawing visitors and archaeologists to the area. But while Angkor Wat has been studied extensively, little was known about what lay in parts of the jungle around the temple.

Scientists suspected that another, older city from the Khmer Empire, known as Mahendraparvata, was

hidden in the tropical forest, based on information they found in old texts. According to the writings, the city was established in 802 on a mountain and served as the Khmer Empire's capital before it moved to Angkor. People had even hiked through the jungle and taken aerial photographs trying to locate the metropolis. They did come across temple ruins, but a city was never found.

Airborne Detectives

In 2012, a team of scientists wanted to investigate about 140 square miles (363 sq km) of the region in search of the remains of Mahendraparvata and other parts of the Khmer Empire. A thick tangle of trees covering the land made exploring such a large area

WAT

During the centuries the temple was abandoned, the roots of trees called strangler figs grew around and under buildings.

Early risers see double at sunrise, when the magnificent morning glow casts a mirror image in the reflecting pool.

ASIA
Gulf of Thailand
CAMBODIA
Tonle Sap
● Angkor Wat
South China Sea

ASIA
Cambodia
INDIAN OCEAN
PACIFIC OCEAN

on foot extremely difficult. So instead, the team took to the skies.

Crisscrossing over forest canopies in a helicopter, archaeologist Damian Evans used an instrument called LIDAR to scan the ground. LIDAR works by rapidly firing off pulses of laser light—up to 200,000 pulses a second. A sensor on the instrument measures how long it takes for each pulse to bounce back from the ground. If a set of laser beams has a shorter return time than the previous pulses sent, it could mean the beams have hit something elevated, such as a building. A longer return time could mean that the beams are bouncing off a low valley or a deep riverbed. Using GPS technology, cartographers then combined all the measurements to

create a digital map of the terrain that revealed mountains, canals, roads, and ruins under the trees.

As the scientists analyzed the map, they noticed an area with a network of roads and canals built into the side of a mountain. It appeared to match the description of Mahendraparvata found in the old texts. Evans and his team knew this had to be the hidden city. "It was a eureka moment," Evans says. Using their map, the team set off to find the old settlement for themselves.

It's a Jungle Out There

The archaeologists started their expedition north of Angkor Wat under the heat of a sizzling sun. They used machetes to cut away tree branches blocking their path, waded knee-deep

in bogs, and dodged dangerous land mines that had been left in the jungle after a war.

Finally, they stumbled on dozens of crumbled temples and evidence of roads and canals, all organized into city blocks. They had reached their destination, and it was indeed Mahendraparvata. And there's more to find—many of the city's artifacts are buried underground.

In the coming years, Evans and his team will continue to investigate the area, and it's likely that more discoveries will be made around Angkor Wat. But just as they did to uncover Mahendraparvata, the scientists will have their work cut out for them. After all, this jungle is very good at keeping secrets.

ZOOMING IN ON ANGKOR WAT

Laser technology was used to create the black-and-white elevation map of the terrain surrounding Angkor Wat (bottom). Then scientists digitally added color and trees to produce a realistic model (top) of the area.

2.4 km

73

America's most popular pizza topping—pepperoni—is practically unheard of in Italy. Order a pepperoni pizza in Naples, and it will arrive covered in bell peppers (*pepperoni* in Italian).

Who invented pizza?

THE EXPERT: Dr. Carol Helstosky, food historian and associate professor of history at the University of Denver

Q: WHERE DID PIZZA COME FROM?

A: That depends on how you define "pizza." The basic definition is that it's a flatbread with toppings baked on it. These go back to ancient Greece, when people cooked flatbreads on hot rocks. But what most people think of as pizza is a sort of pinched out, yeasted flatbread with toppings baked on it. That was developing by the 1700s in Naples, Italy. It wasn't found in the rest of Italy at that time, just Naples. Northern Italians would go to Naples and say, "I tried this really gross food; it was called pizza." They didn't like it at all.

Q: HOW DID PIZZA BECOME THE WORLD-WIDE PHENOMENON IT IS TODAY?

A: Pizza remained isolated in Naples for a really long time, and then suddenly, after 1945, it exploded across the world with remarkable speed. It spread to wherever southern Italians went and lived, including what was referred to in America as the Pizza Belt—between Connecticut, New York, and New Jersey—where quite a few Neapolitans (people from Naples) settled. As legend has it, American soldiers returning home from Europe after World War II had tried pizza and loved it, and they wanted to go to Italian restaurants back home and eat pizza in the United States. That did happen, but probably not with enough regularity to explain pizza's rise. I believe its popularity really spread from the two big chain pizza restaurants, which weren't founded by Italian-Americans!

Q: ARE THERE DIFFERENT STYLES OF PIZZA AROUND THE WORLD?

A: Pizza is very adaptable. For example, in Middle Eastern countries, a chain restaurant makes pizzas with the crust pinched up to hold things, like a little cheeseburger or a chunk of cheese. And of course, toppings vary around the globe. In Naples, which is a seafaring town, they put all these crazy little fish on a pizza. In Russia, they use their traditional ingredients, such as sour cream, potatoes, and caviar. One of my all-time favorites is French fries on pizza. In Japan, pizza is made with potatoes, bacon, and mayonnaise. The history of pizza in Japan is really unique and innovative, with all these interesting ingredients that I don't think we Americans would recognize as pizza. But outside of Italy, Japan has the highest number of certified Neapolitan pizza makers!

Q: WHAT ARE THE INGREDIENTS OF AN AUTHENTIC ITALIAN PIZZA?

A: If you go back to its origins, there was never a strict recipe for a proper pizza. It was always improvised—made out of whatever ingredients and toppings were on hand. That's because pizza started off as fast food. It was street food for working people. It was cheap and filling, and it's always been that way.

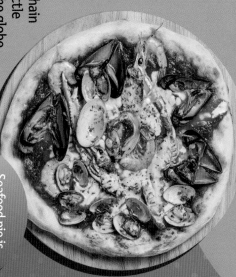

Seafood pie is popular in many places around the world, including Sweden, Russia, and Japan.

ANTICA PIZZERIA

Clever CASTLES

These formidable fortresses have come a long way since they were first built in the early 1000s.

Castles served as homes, strongholds, and symbols of power for mighty monarchs and their lords throughout history. Every last detail about castles was built for defense, from their strategic location, to the materials used to make them, and even to the inclusion of sneaky spaces used for quick getaways.

MAKING AN ENTRANCE

Gatehouse guards were in charge of raising the drawbridge and lowering the portcullis, a heavy gate that protected the front entrance. Gatehouses also had a built-in secret weapon: gaps in the ceiling above the gatehouse allowed defenders to unleash arrows at trespassers and even dump boiling water, hot sand, or other scalding substances on an advancing enemy.

MAGNIFICENT MOATS

Not all castles had them, but some that did filled these deep trenches with up to 30 feet (9 m) of water to keep enemies out. Moats were also used as the castle garbage dump and were a place for emptying toilets. Yuck! Moats that stayed dry were fashioned to be intimidating in other ways: Some were filled with sharp spikes or—in the case of one in the Czech Republic—filled with bears!

COOL CRENELLATIONS

Ever wonder why castles have those rectangular gap-toothed patterns on the tops of their walls and towers? They're called crenellations, and the design isn't just for decoration. Crenellations gave archers a defensive barrier to hide behind and a narrow opening from which they could shoot arrows.

KEEP OUT!

While castles were often built near mountains or rivers as a natural defense against invaders, other castle builders invented ingenious ways to keep their enemies at bay. Designers of Japan's Nijo Castle created squeaky floors to prevent intruders from sneaking in, while Himeji Castle, also in Japan, had a maze-like entrance to confuse enemy attackers.

HIMEJI CASTLE

TOUGH WALLS

Most castle walls consisted of at least two sturdy stone barriers. The outer, or curtain, walls could be up to 30 feet (9 m) high and as thick as a stack of three mattresses! Some went even further: Krak des Chevaliers, a castle in Syria, had walls that were about 80 feet (24 m) thick!

END OF AN ERA

The glory days of castles ended around the 1500s, when cannons became so powerful that stone walls could not withstand them.

KEEPING WATCH

One castle could protect a 10-mile (16-km) radius, so kings often constructed many castles to watch over their realms.

Experts think the Vikings followed this route from Scandinavia (modern-day Denmark, Sweden, and Norway) through the North Atlantic to settle in Newfoundland, Canada.

EUROPE

ICELAND

Greenland

Denmark Strait

ATLANTIC OCEAN

Baffin Bay

Davis Strait

Labrador Sea

Newfoundland

NORTH AMERICA

CANADA

DID VIKINGS EVER

SETTLE IN THE AMERICAS?

A wooden ship heaves onto shore after crossing the Atlantic Ocean to this remote spot. The explorers on board hope to establish a settlement here, in what is now Newfoundland, an island in eastern Canada. They will build homes and repair ships—perhaps preparing for more voyages farther into this unknown land. Who are these mysterious travelers? They are Vikings.

No proof has been found of Viking settlements in North America beyond this spot, called L'Anse aux Meadows. But scientists are working with modern technology in the hope of finding more sites and rewriting Viking history.

SETTING SAIL

"Viking" means "pirate" in Old Norse, and many of these seafarers lived up to the name. Vikings were fierce raiders who lived between 750 and 1050, attacking lands outside their native Scandinavia. Thanks to sleek and speedy ships called longships, they traveled extensively from Afghanistan to Canada, taking control of large areas of Great Britain, Iceland, and France. Their exploits were chronicled in Norse sagas—stories that were fact-based but embellished over centuries of retelling.

FINDING PROOF

In 1960, archaeologists followed descriptions in the sagas to Newfoundland's L'Anse aux Meadows. There they unearthed eight longhouses, a type of building made from timbers and turf that had been found in European Viking settlements. They found buildings used for weaving, ironworking, and ship repair, along with hundreds of artifacts, including bone knitting needles.

The experts concluded L'Anse aux Meadows was the first Viking site in North America.

EYE ON THE SKY

Recently, scientists have enlisted the help of modern high-tech tools in the search for a second Viking outpost. Satellite photos taken from space help scientists look for buried treasure. Viewing Earth from this distance above allows them to see patterns or large structures that aren't visible at eye level. Irregular land surfaces could indicate something buried or hidden by dense growth of plants and trees. Archaeologists have identified areas that deserve further study by scanning aerial images.

VIKING VACATION SPOT?

Baffin Island, north of Newfoundland, is one promising area. Some believe this was a Viking vacation spot referred to as Helluland in the sagas. Excavations on Baffin Island have uncovered whetstones (used to sharpen tools) and other artifacts, including remains of a species of rat that was not native to North America. Research continues.

MORE MYSTERIES

Scientists are still hard at work searching for clues about Viking life in North America. In 2017, experts authenticated a Norse coin that had been found on a beach in Maine. The genuine Norse penny was minted between 1067 and 1093—but how did it land on Maine's shores?

Following the footsteps of the Vikings may take time, but each new discovery is as exciting as the Norse sagas from nearly a thousand years ago.

Viking ships sailed at about the speed you ride your bike.

PECULIAR PREHISTORIC ANIMALS

OUR PLANET'S PAST IS FULL OF WEIRD AND WONDROUS CREATURES. To unlock their secrets, paleontologists study bones and other clues they've left behind. Check out these extraordinary extinct creatures that once stomped, chomped, or swam around this planet.

ARMORED AND ENORMOUS

Well-preserved fossils have given us clues to an enormous armadillo ancestor: *Glyptodon*. This giant armadillo, which lived in Central and South America 10,000 years ago, was the size of a car and weighed up to two tons (1.8 t). It had a thick, bony shell that protected it from nearly any predator. Only a powerful animal like a saber-toothed cat could tip it over to get at its vulnerable belly. *Glyptodon* also had a fringe of spines on its shell to protect its neck, and bony bits embedded on its underside and in its face, which were hard to chomp through. Arguably its best defense was a chubby, spiky tail it could whip around like a club.

LINED WITH SPINES

This tiny, spiny sea creature lived 500 million years ago, was less than an inch (2.5 cm) long, and thinner than a single hair. The first paleontologist to seriously study it in fossil form believed that the odd creature walked on stiltlike spines and grasped food with its tentacles. Named *Hallucigenia* (from Latin for "hallucination" or "illusion"), this tiny wormlike creature with seven wiggling spines and tentacles seemed like something from a dream. After studying a fossil of a similar creature called *Microdictyon*, scientists realized they had been studying *Hallucigenia* upside down! The spines actually lined its back, and the "tentacles" turned out to be spindly legs.

BUZZ-SAW JAWS

Helicoprion had a saw for a jaw. But its lower jaw didn't spin like the circular blade in a table saw. Instead, *Helicoprion* would snap its spiral-shaped lower jaw closed in an instant to slice though yummy soft squid. The backward movement of the closing curved jaw pushed the food to the back of its throat, as if it were on a conveyor belt. In its day—about 270 million years ago—this fearsome feeder reached sizes of up to 20 to 25 feet (6 to 7.6 m) long—a little longer than a modern great white shark.

MEGA BEAST

It looked like a sloth, acted like a sloth, but was too huge to climb a tree. The ancient giant ground sloth, called *Megatherium*, was about the size of an elephant and roamed the Paleolithic Americas alongside early humans. Like its modern-day relatives, *Megatherium* had massive claws, but it was no predator; it had the teeth of a plant-eater. The claws probably came in handy when pulling a favorite treat—avocados—off a tree branch.

FIERCE AND FAST

This bird didn't fly, but it didn't need to. At about 10 feet (3 m) tall, *Gastornis* towered over most other creatures of North America and Europe during the Paleocene and Eocene periods some 50 million years ago. Its wings were too small for liftoff, but its long legs helped *Gastornis* reach speeds of up to 30 miles an hour (48 km/h). Some experts think it could run much faster and could outpace a cheetah, if it were alive today. But for all its brawn, this bird was no bully. Studies show it ate mainly a diet of hard fruits and seeds.

EXTREME FASHION

THROUGHOUT HISTORY PEOPLE HAVE GONE TO AMAZING LENGTHS TO BE FASHIONABLE. FROM SUPERSIZE SKIRTS TO ELFIN SHOES, FASHION TRENDS SET THE STYLE OF THE TIMES, SERVED USEFUL PURPOSES, AND KEPT TRADITIONS ALIVE. TRY ON THESE TRENDS FOR SIZE.

STANDING TALL

Stilts: not just for the circus! These high-stepping accessories were part of daily life for some shepherds of the past. There were few roads in the swamplands of 19th-century Landes, France. To get around without sinking into the soggy soil, shepherds took to walking on stilts. Called *tchangues* ("big legs"), wooden poles strapped to the wearer's legs gave him a bird's-eye view of his flock. A third pole served as a support, like a crutch, to prop up the shepherd when he needed a rest. Completing the shepherd's costume was a shaggy sheepskin vest, canvas leggings, and a beret. Practical *and* stylish!

THE MANE EVENT

History is filled with head-turning hairstyles, but this one is tops. Worn by the Changjiao Miao of China's Guizhou Province, the longhorn headdress resembles a pair of bull horns. According to legend, farmers fastened false horns to their heads to frighten away wild animals that threatened crops and livestock. Today, black wool woven with real hair from ancestors is coiled around a boomerang-shaped wooden comb and tied to the head with white fabric. This heavy headgear can weigh up to 13 pounds (6 kg). Miao women wear it during festivals and other special occasions.

RUFFING IT

When a collar called the ruff first came into fashion, it was a simple accessory a few inches wide. But during the rule of Queen Elizabeth I in the late 1500s, ruffs grew bigger ... and bigger ... and bigger ... Finally, they were so enormous that people had to manufacture special long-handled utensils just to eat their supper! To get the perfect pouf, white fabric was stiffened with starch and pressed into pleats. The ruff's pleats were tightly folded, so when extended, the ruff fabric would be as much as 19 feet (6 m) long! Following fashion trends can be *ruff*!

WHY SO WIDE?

Try going for a twirl in this sweeping skirt! This voluminous look became all the rage in 18th-century Europe when Marie Antoinette, who had a passion for fashion, was queen of France. It was made possible by an undergarment called panniers, which consisted of two hoops belted to the sides of the waist. Unfortunately, ladies often had to walk sideways to fit through doorways. This fashion fad eventually fell from favor, but it inspired the name for the storage bags on either side of the rear wheel of a bike, also called panniers.

WIG-TASTIC SMELLS

Egypt was famous for its exotic perfumes. But forget just dabbing a scent on your wrists—ancient Egyptians took smell to a whole new extreme. Archaeologists uncovered art showing both men and women wearing cones atop their heads at feasts. Hieroglyphs (ancient Egyptian writing) reveal that these cones were made of heavily perfumed wax or grease. The soft cones would slowly melt into the wearer's wig or hair, filling the air with an enchanting aroma. As a bonus, the cones served as a time-release deodorant, masking stinky body odor.

GET TO THE POINT

Crakows were named for the Polish capital, Krakow, where pointy shoes were the height of medieval fashion. These flat-soled shoes were made of leather, silk, or other soft materials, and toe points were stuffed with moss or wool to hold their shape. To avoid tripping, some people tied their toe tips to their knees with fancy metal chains. Eventually, laws were passed to limit toe length to two inches (5 cm). It must have been tough to toe the line of this trend!

83

Planners originally wanted to paint San Francisco's

GOLDEN GATE BRIDGE

black with yellow stripes.

WHY ISN'T THIS FAMOUS BRIDGE THE COLOR OF A BUMBLEBEE?

The suspension bridge (an overpass held up by cables connected to towers) is one of the oldest forms of engineering. The earliest ones consisted of vines, twisted grasses, or woven bamboo connecting two pieces of land.

The Golden Gate Bridge in San Francisco, California, U.S.A., is a real trailblazer. Finished in 1937, it was the first bridge to have one of its supporting columns built right in the open ocean. Builders worked above and below the sea, enduring harsh winds and choppy waters. Despite the tough conditions, they succeeded in constructing what was then the world's longest suspension bridge.

The U.S. Navy worried about the Golden Gate's visibility in the famously foggy bay; the mariners proposed painting the steel black with yellow stripes. But when the steel arrived, it was coated in an orange-red primer to prevent corrosion. The architect liked the color so much that he decided to keep it. The hue, known as international orange, makes the Golden Gate instantly recognizable, and one of the most photographed sites in North America.

SECRETS of POMPEII

When canal diggers in southern Italy in the 1590s accidentally unearthed fragments of marble inscribed with Latin text, they had no clue they were standing on the ruins of the ancient Roman city of Pompeii. Excavation of the site wouldn't begin for more than 150 years, but when it did, Pompeii's rediscovery rocked the world. This long-forgotten city had been buried under millions of tons of volcanic ash following the eruption of Mount Vesuvius in the first century A.D. The same layers of ash that buried the city also preserved it, and today, it is the most continuously excavated place in the world, offering a rare window into the lives of ancient Romans.

Frozen in Time

Pompeii was located by the base of Mount Vesuvius, near the modern city of Naples, a rich agricultural area. When Pompeiians awoke on August 24, 79, they were likely in a festive mood. It was the morning after Vulcania, an annual festival honoring Vulcan, the Roman god of fire. (The word "volcano" comes from Vulcan.) But by midday, Pompeii would be changed forever. That's when Mount Vesuvius, silent for nearly 2,000 years, roared back to life, shooting ash and smoke 20 miles (32 km) into the air.

Some people ran for their lives, clutching their valuables. Others took shelter in their homes. Around midnight, about 12 hours after the first eruption, Vesuvius exploded again. Surges of ash, pumice, rock, and toxic gas rushed down the mountainside. Traveling toward Pompeii at up to 180 miles an hour (290 km/h), it scorched everything in its path. By the next morning, the city, along with many of its citizens, had been completely swallowed up.

Revealed in the Ruins

Excavations at Pompeii have revealed many secrets of this Roman town. Unearthed buildings include magnificent villas of its wealthiest citizens, homes of tradespeople, one-room workshops, an inn for travelers, an amphitheater for chariot races, public baths, and two theaters. Well-paved streets had high sidewalks and stepping-stones to keep pedestrians out of the mud.

Discoveries at the site show that wealthier residents lived in lavish homes with elaborate gardens and stately fountains. Of note is a well-preserved room, discovered recently, known as The Enchanted Garden. Thought to be a place of worship, it contains a raised pool surrounded by walls adorned with richly colored frescoes (murals painted on plaster). One fresco is a clever optical illusion—a lifelike peacock painted to appear as if it is walking in an actual garden. And treasure chests hidden away in homes unlocked more discoveries of daily life: jewelry, coins, and silverware.

Taking a Bite Out of History

From excavated evidence, frescoes, and writings, historians have learned about the foods Pompeiians ate, some of which might be familiar today: fish from local waters, olives, grilled meats and vegetables, grains, nuts, and peaches. A kind of fast food was served at snack bars called thermopolia, where bread with salted fish, baked cheese, and lentils could make a quick meal.

An excavated bakery was found with loaves of bread still in it—2,000 years old and carbonized (turned to charcoal), possibly the oldest ever discovered! Pompeiians were especially fond of a sauce made from fermented fish guts called garum. They ate it themselves, and it was a pricey delicacy they sold in trade. In fact, one of the wealthiest residents of Pompeii was a fish sauce tycoon of the time.

The rediscovery of Pompeii has revealed many clues about ancient Roman life, including how people lived and, tragically, how many died in Vesuvius's violent eruption nearly two thousand years ago. Astonishing artwork and artifacts that might have faded or crumbled over time were preserved, and its people live on through the secrets the city of Pompeii continues to reveal.

Mount Vesuvius rises 4,203 feet (1,281 m) along the Bay of Naples. Adventurous hikers can climb to the summit and peer into the open crater.

Volcanic ash settled around the victims at the moment of death. When the bodies decayed, holes remained inside the solid ash. Scientists poured plaster into the holes to preserve the shapes of the victims.

AN IMPORTANT DISCOVERY

A few days after Vesuvius destroyed Pompeii, it erupted again, covering nearby Herculaneum. This wealthy village by the sea was smaller than Pompeii, and most of its residents had time to flee before it was buried in 60 feet (18 m) of mostly lava and mud. Unlike the heat and ash in Pompeii, the mud preserved organic materials like wood, textiles, and papers.

One of the most significant finds in Herculaneum so far is the Villa of Papyri. Considered one of the most luxurious Roman homes of its day, it had a 200-foot (61-m)-long swimming pool, massive columns, bronzes, and marble statues. It also contained a huge library of ancient papyri (texts). This treasure trove was rescued in the 1700s and is now housed in several museums, including the National Library of Naples.

CHAPTER 5

SHOCKING SCIENCE

The universe is a dynamic place full of explosive chemical reactions, elements constantly combining and recombining, precious metals with extraordinary properties, and amazing cosmic displays in the night sky. We aren't just viewers watching a spectacular show; all of us are curious scientists who want to know *why*. Read on to learn more about the inner mechanics of how things work, from deep inside the human body to the outer reaches of our galaxy—and more shocking science secrets.

The VISORS on astronauts' helmets are coated with a thin layer of GOLD.

While gold may be blindingly beautiful, engineers are able to make it into a thin enough coating that the precious metal doesn't get in the way of the astronauts' vision. Instead, this clever coating filters out harmful ultraviolet rays from the sun, protecting the astronauts' eyes. Engineers also drape gold foil over spacecraft and satellites to prevent the vehicles from overheating in outer space. This works because gold has remarkable powers of reflection: Up to 99 percent of damaging infrared light and more than half of the visible and ultraviolet light that hits it bounces away. This means sunlight doesn't have a chance to heat up the interior of the spacecraft. Now that's cool!

Because gold is so reflective, NASA is building a telescope with a giant golden mirror inside. The mirror of the James Webb Space Telescope is 21 feet (6.4 m) wide, and its 18 segments are sprayed with a thin layer of pure gold. At a price tag of $8.8 billion, it is the gold standard of telescopes. That is some super high-tech space bling!

That's SUPER COOL!

AWESOME ALTERNATIVE ENERGY

WHEN YOU THINK OF ALTERNATIVE ENERGY, WIND FARMS OR SOLAR PANELS MIGHT COME TO MIND. THESE RENEWABLE RESOURCES ARE FRIENDLIER TO THE ENVIRONMENT THAN TRADITIONAL ENERGY SOURCES, SUCH AS NATURAL GAS, OIL, AND COAL. BUT THERE ARE OTHER, MORE OFFBEAT OPTIONS YOU MAY NOT HAVE HEARD OF. DISCOVER SIX ELECTRIFYING NEW ENERGY INNOVATIONS.

A STEP AHEAD

A British company has invented a floor tile that converts footsteps into energy. As people walk across the tiles, the pressure from their feet pushes on tiny generators below the surface. The generators spin, creating electricity. These high-tech tiles have been installed in airports, schools, and retail centers around the world. Now that's power walking!

MIGHTY MOO-VERS

No, this cow isn't heading to school. Designed by scientists in Argentina, this sporty backpack gathers a cow's gassy emissions. Cows produce an enormous amount of methane—a greenhouse gas that's a major contributor to climate change—as they digest the food they eat. Researchers are studying how captured cow gas could be converted into energy. One idea could have us saying, "Moo-ove over, fuel pump": A cow generates enough methane in a single day to power a car for 24 hours.

BELLY BACTERIA

Doctors have long known that the bacteria living inside our stomach and intestines are important to our health. But one study came to a truly shocking conclusion: "Gut bugs" also generate electricity! Don't plug a phone charger into your belly button just yet. Engineers will need to invent bacteria-powered batteries to harness this unique energy.

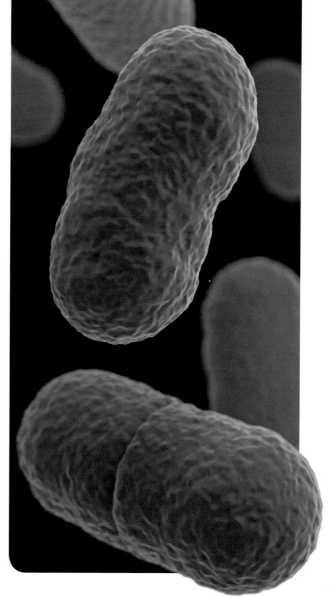

POOP POWER

In Cambridge, Massachusetts, U.S.A., dog poop lights up the night sky, thanks to a special streetlamp. Pet owners plop Rover's business into a box at the base of the lamppost and crank a handle. The box is a biodigester—like a compost bin—in which waste is broken down by bacteria. The regular deposits are converted to a gas that powers the streetlight. What a bright idea!

TOTALLY TOFU

In Indonesia, tofu isn't just food, it's also fuel. The village of Kalisari is testing a clean energy program that turns water left over from the tofu-making process into a renewable energy source called biogas. Biogas is produced when food, plants, manure, or other organic matter break down without oxygen. Piped into local homes to run stoves and ovens, biogas is a cheap alternative to traditional cooking fuel. The system also reduces environmental pollution. Since about 250 villagers make tofu for a living, Kalisari is the perfect place to test tofu power.

EEL-ECTRIC

It's no secret that electric eels produce energy—it's right in their name. As an experiment, staff at an aquarium in Utah, U.S.A., attached electrodes to the sides of a tank to collect electricity emitted by the tank's occupant—an electric eel named Sparky—from the water. They were able to capture enough voltage to make Christmas lights twinkle every time Sparky moved. The aquarium experiment may be important for future science. Biophysicists are trying to develop new power sources that mimic the way electric eel cells produce electricity. They could replace the batteries in medical implants such as pacemakers.

INCREDIBLE TECH

PLANES FASTER THAN THE SPEED OF SOUND! DRONES THE SIZE OF A PENNY! DOORS THAT UNLOCK WITH YOUR HEARTBEAT!

Discover five new cutting-edge technologies that are even cooler than science fiction.

BIONIC PROSTHESES

A prosthesis is an artificial limb, like an arm or leg, that people can wear if they don't have a natural limb. For many years, prostheses were mechanical devices that lacked a sense of touch. By operating something like a pulley system on their shoulders, people could open or close prosthetic hands, but they couldn't tell how strongly they were grabbing something. They broke a lot of eggs and delivered some crushing handshakes. But researchers have recently developed a bionic prosthesis wired directly into the nerves on someone's arm. It can send signals to the person's brain and be controlled like a natural hand. Now people with high-tech prosthetic hands can even feel textures and enjoy holding hands.

X-PLANE

The X-plane is a super-streamlined experimental jet that NASA and Lockheed Martin are developing to carry passengers over land faster than the speed of sound, about 767 miles an hour (1,234 km/h). Supersonic passenger travel over land has faced a serious challenge: sonic booms. These are the huge, thunderlike cracks created by shock waves, which are rapid changes in pressure at supersonic speeds. They're not just annoying; they can damage property on the ground. So NASA is trying a new technology in the X-plane that limits the effect to a soft thump instead of a big boom. In fact, the X-plane's formal name is Quiet Supersonic Transport, or QueSST.

ROBOBEES

These teeny tiny drones are built by Nat Geo Explorer and electrical engineer Robert Wood. While they may be small, Wood has some big dreams for these robotic bees: The insect-size bots might one day help with real-life rescue operations. Wood hopes the RoboBees will eventually be able to zoom into places that would be difficult or dangerous for humans to access. For instance, they could fly into collapsed buildings and help find injured people. If that wasn't cool enough, the drones won't use voice commands or even be controlled by a joystick. Instead, they'll fly by themselves, with heat-seeking sensors to find survivors and preprogrammed commands to avoid bumping into walls. When they find what they're after, they'll wirelessly send a message.

SMART GLASSES

Smart glasses like Spectacles by Snapchat are wearable computers that look like regular eyeglasses with a small camera in the corner. They're wirelessly connected to the internet and can take photos or videos. Pressing a button on the frame triggers a sensor to start recording the world from your perspective, completely hands-free. Smart glasses aren't just for social media. Some factory workers wear them so they can read instructions while keeping their hands free to assemble products. They're also used by some doctors, who can wirelessly send live video of their appointments to an assistant in a different location. The assistant takes notes, so the doctor is free to focus on the patients.

FINGERPRINT-ENABLED WRISTBAND

Want to unlock your front door? No key required! This fingerprint-enabled wristband has it covered! How does it work? The Nymi Band has a security token inside that is unique to the wearer. Put the band on your wrist and press your finger on top, and it reads your unique fingerprint to activate the band. The Nymi Band acts as your password to wirelessly unlock computers and open doors that have been paired with it.

sailing STONES

>>> Imagine seeing a track in a dry bed of mud with a heavy stone at the end. It looks as if the rock moved across the flat land on its own. But how could that be possible? In California, U.S.A., Death Valley's "sailing stones" weigh as much as 700 pounds (320 kg), and they move all by themselves. There are no footprints, tire tracks, or other signs of human intervention. These rocks sometimes sit still for decades, then sail off to a new location.

SLIDE AND GO SEEK

Scientists have been trying for 100 years to figure out how the rocks move. One theory was that wind blew the stones when the lake bed was muddy and slick. Another was that the rocks were pushed by the wind over large sheets of ice.

BREAKING AWAY

The sailing stones form when rocks break off the mountains around Death Valley, roll down into the low-lying valley, and settle atop the Racetrack Playa.

MINI TO MIGHTY

The sailing stones can range in size from tiny pebbles to large boulders weighing as much as 400 bowling balls! When the stones move, they leave tracks up to 600 feet (183 m) long.

MYSTERY SOLVED

Scientists turned to GPS tags and time-lapse photography to try to capture the sailing stones in action. And it worked! Their study finally revealed the mechanism behind the movement: a perfect storm of water, ice, sun, and wind. First, a rare rainstorm drenches the dry lake bed. Then, the valley freezes over. The morning sun begins to melt the ice. Large sheets break off and drift across the slick surface. Gusts of wind shove the ice masses against the stones, pushing them forward. The mysterious tracks in the mud remain until the next rain, when they'll be off to the races again!

RACETRACK PLAYA

While the lake bed known as the Racetrack Playa is dry most of the time, during brief rainy seasons a shallow layer of water covers it. When the water evaporates, the mud dries and cracks into small hexagonal shapes.

LOWS AND HIGHS

Death Valley is the largest national park in the lower 48 states of the United States. At 282 feet (86 m) below sea level, it is also the lowest point in North America. With the hottest air temperature on the planet, summers are known to top out at a scorching 120°F (49°C).

THE PROBLEM
WITH PLASTIC

A plastic bag was discovered in the Mariana Trench, 36,000 feet (10,972 m) below the ocean's surface.

Plastic water bottles, straws, and bags are a part of our everyday lives, but these single-use items don't disappear when you're done with them. Unlike paper or food waste, plastic doesn't decompose, or break down into pieces that can be reused by nature. That means it stays around forever. And most of it ends up in the ocean, causing major problems for wildlife.

Luckily, humans are pitching in to study the issues and look for solutions in the fight to reduce plastic waste.

A GROWING PROBLEM

Waste management expert, environmental engineer, and National Geographic Explorer Dr. Jenna Jambeck did the math: Today, nearly 9 million tons (8.1 million t) of plastic ends up in the world's oceans every year—as much as if you stacked five plastic grocery bags full of trash on top of each other on every foot (0.3 m) of coastline in the world.

How does it get there? Plastic left on the ground as litter often blows into creeks and rivers, eventually ending up in the ocean. And often, plastic doesn't go it alone.

PATCHES OF PLASTIC

Patches are places in our ocean where plastic accumulates. The largest concentration, called the Great Pacific Garbage Patch, is located in the Pacific Ocean between California and Hawaii, U.S.A., weighs as much as 43,000 cars, and covers an area twice the size of Texas.

While it sounds like a place where you could walk on top of the debris, in reality, you could drive a boat through the patch and not see much at all. That's because 94 percent of the 1.8 trillion pieces of plastic in the patch are microplastics—tiny particles smaller than a sesame seed. Some microplastics were made on purpose—for toothpaste or cosmetics products, for instance—while others came from larger pieces of plastic that have worn down over time. Microplastics are bad news for animals: When they eat them, they can get sick. And when fish eat them, and then we eat fish... well, we're eating plastic, too.

POLLUTION SOLUTIONS

From organizing beach cleanups to tackling the Great Pacific Garbage Patch, lots of people are brainstorming ways to remove ocean debris. Some scientists, like Dr. Jambeck, aim to track trash to its source. To do that, Jambeck created the Marine Debris Tracker, a smartphone app that allows users to log litter items they find. The goal is to rapidly assemble litter data so that scientists and crews can use the information for more efficient cleanups.

Cities and communities around the world are trying their own solutions. In Baltimore, Maryland, U.S.A., a googly-eyed machine named Mr. Trash Wheel sits in the city's harbor. The water's current turns the wheel, which picks up floating trash and loads it into the large container behind it. The trash collected is then hauled away and burned to power nearby homes.

The plastic problem is one that humans will be dealing with for years to come. It will take lots of ideas and people working together to protect ocean animals and keep Earth clean.

kids vs. PLASTIC

The problems of plastic often seem so big that it's hard to believe one person can make a difference. But little actions add up, and there are plenty of ways to help. First, grab a parent and head to *natgeokids.com/ kidsvsplastic* to take the Kids vs. Plastic pledge and get your Planet Protector certificate. There's also information about the effects of plastic, tips, and projects to help reduce your plastic use. By understanding the issue and taking action, you can help stop the plastic problem.

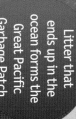

Litter that ends up in the ocean forms the Great Pacific Garbage Patch.

Great Pacific Garbage Patch

PACIFIC OCEAN

NORTH AMERICA

SOUTH AMERICA

ATLANTIC OCEAN

EUROPE

AFRICA

ARCTIC OCEAN

ASIA

INDIAN OCEAN

AUSTRALIA

ANTARCTICA

PACIFIC OCEAN

Volunteers removed nearly 100 million pieces of plastic and more from coastal areas around the world in a single day during an international cleanup effort in 2018. Weird finds included a sled, a tractor, ties, a toy tiara, and a full-size car!

The world's largest amethyst geode is named the Empress of Uruguay (where it was found). It's about 11 feet (3.4 m) tall and weighs 5,500 pounds (2,500 kg). That's one big February birthstone!

what is a crystal?

THE EXPERT: Dr. Aaron Celestian, curator of mineral sciences for the Natural History Museum of Los Angeles County

Q: WHAT ARE CRYSTALS, AND WHAT MAKES THEM SPECIAL?

A: A crystal is a solid material that contains a repeating pattern of atoms over three dimensions. If you had a whole bunch of marbles on the table, and you took your time to align them so they were stacked on top of one another, you would see a pattern start to develop, like in a crystal. But if you just took the marbles and squished them together, they'd be randomly arranged. That gives you a good idea of the difference between a crystal and other types of materials. Crystals are all around us. Salt is a crystal, sugar is a crystal, there are crystals in our bodies, crystals in the dirt we walk on ... they're everywhere. Crystallography (the study of crystals) is an interesting field because there is so much about our planet and ourselves that is crystalline (has the structure of a crystal), and a lot of things need crystals to live and to function. One of the things we're looking at now is how crystals can harbor life for many millions of years.

Q: SO CRYSTALS ARE LIKE TINY TIME CAPSULES?

A: Yes, they are. We find crystals with bacteria trapped in them. As a crystal grows, little pockets of fluid get trapped inside and the crystal keeps growing. The fluid is entombed inside the crystal. There are crystals from Mexico, at least 50,000 years old, that contain hibernating bacteria, which you can rejuvenate by adding water. It's crazy how long these bacteria can live! Definitely millions of years, perhaps even hundreds of millions of years.

Q: WHAT CAN CRYSTALS TELL US ABOUT THE FUTURE?

A: If you know how crystals formed and changed in the past and what drove those changes, then you can see how crystals are forming now and take that information and use it for the future. You could say, "I see how this crystal is changing, or how this series of crystals are changing over time; that's going to tell me what life is going to be like and what our planet could be like a hundred years from now or a thousand years from now."

Q: WHAT ELSE CAN CRYSTALS TELL US?

A: One of the crystals we are looking at is halite—regular old table salt. Halite forms when a lake evaporates. If we go to a different planet and find halite, then we can say that there was once water there. We apply our understanding of how halite forms on Earth to other planets.

The next spacecraft heading to Mars will explore a place called Jezero Crater. The craft will use a laser spectrometer to look for signs of life there; lasers fired from the spectrometer can detect the type of molecules inside a material. Maybe we'll find out that Jezero used to be a lake.

If you heat up a zeolite, water will leak out of it. "Zeolite" is Greek for "boiling rock." When the zeolite begins to cool, it will soak up the water like a sponge.

Brilliantly colored vanadinite occurs only with other minerals, including barite (shown here).

"TALK"
with animals.

Plants use
smell and color to

That's SUPER
COOL!

STANDING OUT IN A CROWD

"Pick me, pick me!" If a berry could talk, that's what it would say to a hungry bird or monkey. Many fruit-bearing plants rely on animals to spread their seeds—the farther the better. A fruit that falls at the base of a tree may sprout a seedling, but for a plant species to truly thrive, it needs to stake out new ground. How can a plant stand out in a forest that looks like a big, delicious bowl of salad? Actual speech is out of the question, so plants rely on color and fragrance to get attention. It's part of what scientists call an evolved communication system.

The fruit of one African tree smells like sweaty gym socks. The tree didn't forget to do its laundry—the smell has a purpose. The odor attracts forest elephants. Other creatures destroy the seeds when they eat them, but a pachyderm will swallow the seed whole. When the elephant "deposits" the seed somewhere else, a new tree gets "planted." Most of Madagascar's lemurs are red-green colorblind, so ripe fruit in their territory has evolved to be yellow, a color they can see more easily. And when foxes eat berries and cherries, the seeds pass through their digestive system intact, exiting with a bonus dose of dung fertilizer. It's a win-win: The fox gets a meal, and the fruit gets a new territory.

BOOM! BANG! BLING!

SECRETS ⟫⟫⟫ of FIREWORKS

If you want to have a blast for your celebration, there have to be fireworks! What's better than a dark summer night popping with a dozen different bright colors, and that well-known crackling sound as the shower of color reaches its peak in the sky. Oh, and those booms—sudden bursts of sound that you don't quite expect. It all adds up to an explosive experience. But how are these colors and sounds made? It's all about chemistry.

Chemistry in Action

The fiery drama begins in a steel tube called a mortar. The mortar's bottom compartment is filled with the basic formula for gunpowder, invented in China nearly 2,000 years ago: charcoal, potassium nitrate, and sulfur. A fuse is packed into the powder. Then a shell is added.

It's actually the shell for fireworks that contains the razzle-dazzle. Pellets called stars are packed into the shell. These stars are made from metals and minerals in combinations that create certain colors and sounds. Other effects, like the shape of a firework in the sky, depend on how the stars are arranged in the shell. Firework shapes can be long and gently curved like a shooting star or rounded for an oval shape, or burst out from a center point like a flower blooming.

Now it's showtime! The fuses are lit. The first fuse, in the bottom of the mortar, launches the shell into the air; the second fuse blows when the shell is airborne, igniting the bling. Bright colors and crackling sounds light up the night. What a blast!

Color Wheel in the Sky

The metals and minerals bound together to form the stars come in a wide array of blues, reds, whites, golds, yellows, greens, and purples. Red comes

Fireworks displays can be seen at celebrations around the world, including on New Year's Eve in London.

from the chemical strontium, and yellow is made with sodium. Calcium—the same stuff that makes our bones strong—is used to make orange fireworks. For a shower of blue, copper is the mineral needed. So, naturally, purple is a mixture of strontium and copper. The white flashes are made with aluminum and magnesium.

It takes hundreds of mortars to pull off a major fireworks display like the annual Independence Day celebration at the National Mall in Washington, D.C. The blasts for this display reach 300 to 600 feet (91 to 183 m) in the air, high above the monuments and spectators below.

CALL IN THE EXPERTS

Fireworks displays are serious business. It takes trained professionals called pyrotechnicians to pull off a fabulous—and safe—sky show. Pyrotechnicians are skilled in controlling explosive devices and doing it safely. They know how to set up a fireworks display so that everything goes off with a bang—in the air. They maximize the wow factor by placing and pacing the blasting shells for the biggest effects possible. Imagine planning all that and *also* timing it to music!

Also called pyrotechnics, fireworks are like paintings in the sky ... literally! The word comes from the Greek for fire (*pyr*) and art (*techne*).

FIREWORKS COLOR CHEMISTRY

Mix these elements in a firework, and you'll have a rainbow of colored sparks!

Sr STRONTIUM	**+ Li** LITHIUM	**= RED**
Ca CALCIUM	**+ Cl** CHLORINE	**= ORANGE**
Na SODIUM	**+ Cl** CHLORINE	**= YELLOW**
Ba BARIUM	**+ Cl** CHLORINE	**= GREEN**
Cu COPPER	**+ Cl** CHLORINE	**= BLUE**
Sr STRONTIUM	**+ Cu** COPPER	**= PURPLE**

105

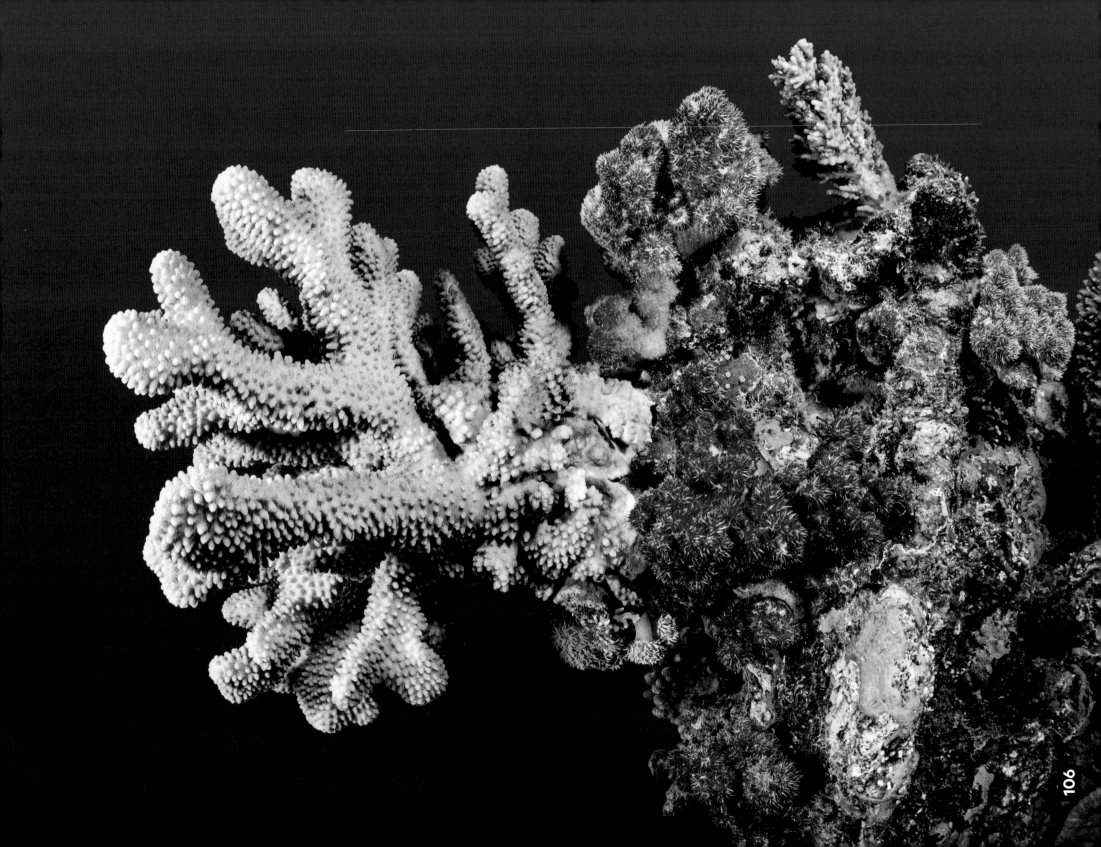

PECULIAR PLANET

What would you call a planet that's full of liquid rock, covered in alien-looking landscapes, and populated by animals that glow in the dark? Earth! This spectacular sphere we call home has accumulated scores of strange secrets in its 4.5 billion years of history. It can transform minerals into priceless gems, create candy-colored mountains, and blast plumes of boiling water hundreds of feet high. Some of Earth's mysteries are buried below its surface, while others are swirling in the skies, and still more are hidden in plain sight.

Some **sand dunes** sound like they're **WHISTLING** and **SINGING.**

WHAT CAUSES THIS SANDY SYMPHONY?

When explorer Marco Polo described hearing musical sounds coming from the sand dunes of the Gobi desert more than 700 years ago, he could not come up with an explanation. What causes the incredible singing, whistling, and even booming heard in the Gobi, which stretches across northern China into Mongolia? To get to the bottom of this mystery, scientists had to use *their bottoms*—literally—by sliding down the dunes. This field-work caused mini-avalanches that unleashed a desert melody.

Not all dunes perform this way. Singing dunes are tall—150 feet (46 m) or more. The top layer of sand must be loose and dry. Below the loose layer, there is a damp, hard-packed layer. When wind hits the dry sand, it can cause an avalanche. The top layer of sand vibrates as it slides down, creating sound that is amplified by the firm inner layer. Another factor at play is that the sand grains must be about the same size. Experts think that the equal-size grains shuffle down at the same speed, creating a clear tone. If you're ever in a sandy desert, keep an ear out: Singing dunes can be heard from miles away.

SECRETS of a BLUE

The night is pitch black. But the dark slopes of a hill inside the crater of Kawah Ijen volcano in Indonesia, a country in Asia, are lit up like a holiday light show. Tourists flock to the volcano to see what look like glowing rivers of blue lava. But they aren't rivers of lava. They're rivers of glowing sulfur.

Burning Blue

Glowing red lava flowing from an erupting volcano isn't unusual. Glowing sulfur is. Hot, sulfur-rich gases escape constantly from cracks called fumaroles in Kawah Ijen's crater. The gases cool when they hit the air.

Some condense into liquid sulfur, which flows down the hillside. When the sulfur and leftover gases ignite, they burn bright blue and light up the sky.

Scientists were told that sulfur miners on the volcano sometimes use torches to ignite the sulfur. The blue flames make Kawah Ijen popular with tourists, who watch from a safe distance. Recently, scientists confirmed that some of the sulfur and gases also burn naturally, igniting as the hot gases combine with oxygen in the air.

Volcano Miners

Sulfur is a common volcanic gas, and its chemical properties make it useful

in the manufacture of many things, such as rubber. It's so plentiful in Kawah Ijen's crater that miners make a dangerous daily trek into the crater to collect it from a fumarole near an acid lake.

"The local people pipe the gases from the fumarole through ceramic pipes," says John Pallister, a geologist with the Cascades Volcano Observatory in Washington State, U.S.A. He has walked into the crater himself, wearing a gas mask for protection against the clouds of acid that rise from the lake. "They spray the pipes with water from a spring," he says. "This cools the gases and causes them to condense into

Electric blue lava lights up the night sky as it pours down the volcano's sides.

VOLCANO

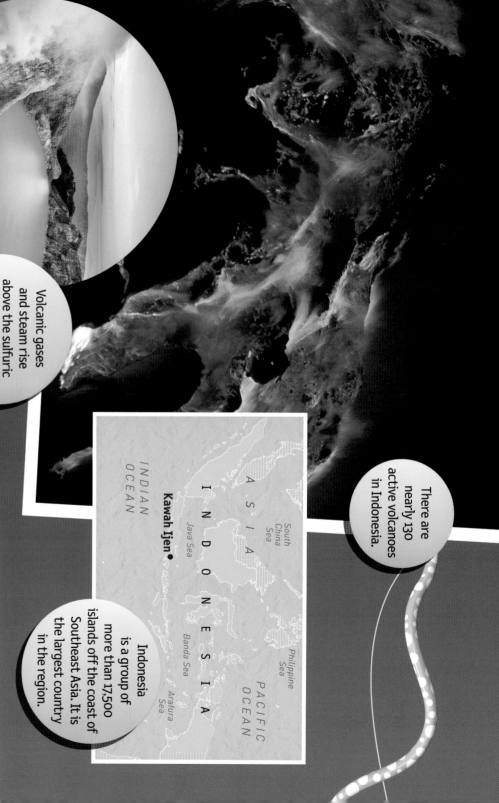

molten sulfur. The sulfur then cools and hardens into rock.

Using this method, miners get more usable rock faster than if they just collected scattered pieces. They smash up the rock with metal bars, stuff the pieces into baskets, and carry them out of the crater on their backs. The loads are heavy—between 100 and 200 pounds (45 to 90 kg) apiece.

Reading the Danger Zone

Miners face another danger: a huge eruption. Kawah Ijen's last big eruption was almost 200 years ago, but the volcano is still active. A big eruption could endanger miners and tourists.

Indonesian scientists want to find a way to predict a big eruption in time to keep everyone safe. But the deep acid lake makes it difficult to pick up the usual signals that warn of a coming volcanic eruption.

For example, certain gases are usually more abundant right before an eruption. But in this lake, these gases dissolve in the deep liquid before they can register on the geologists' monitoring equipment.

As scientists search for ways to predict this unusual volcano's behavior, Kawah Ijen's blue fires continue to attract audiences who appreciate the volcano's amazing glow.

Volcanic gases and steam rise above the sulfuric water in the volcano's crater—the world's largest acid lake.

There are nearly 130 active volcanoes in Indonesia.

Indonesia is a group of more than 17,500 islands off the coast of Southeast Asia. It is the largest country in the region.

HOW KAWAH IJEN ERUPTS

SUBDUCTION ZONE

OCEAN

AUSTRALIAN PLATE

EURASIAN PLATE

MAGMA

Earth's outer shell is broken into a jigsaw puzzle of several tectonic plates, or gigantic slabs of rock, that move constantly. In Indonesia, the oceanic Australian plate slips under the Eurasian plate at a subduction zone. As the Australian plate slides deep down, heat generated in Earth's interior makes the plate superhot, and parts of it melt. This melted rock, called magma, rises toward Earth's surface. Pressure on the magma lessens as it rises, allowing gases inside to expand, which can lead to explosive volcanic eruptions.

INDIAN OCEAN

ASIA

INDONESIA

Kawah Ijen

South China Sea

Philippine Sea

Java Sea

Banda Sea

Arafura Sea

PACIFIC OCEAN

GEYSERS

COOL!

Like volcanoes, geysers erupt—but instead of lava, they send jets of boiling water and steam into the air. The most common are fountain geysers, which have a large vent. Strokkur (shown), one of Iceland's best known geysers, is this type. Rather than shooting a stream straight up, they usually spew in all directions.

GALACTIC GEYSERS

Geysers aren't just an Earth phenomenon. NASA scientists have charted at least 101 geysers on the surface of Enceladus, one of Saturn's larger moons. These geysers spew plumes of water vapor and ice particles into space—some reaching as far as Saturn's outer ring. Jupiter's moon Europa may also have geysers, according to recent research.

EUROPA

FOUL FUMAROLES

Fumaroles don't erupt, but these vents release steam and gases, such as sulfur dioxide and carbon dioxide. This gives the smoky emissions a strong, stinky, rotten-egg smell. Ew!

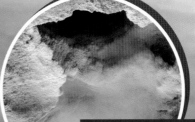

OLD FAITHFUL

The world's most famous geyser was named for its predictable pattern of eruptions. Every 60 to 110 minutes, Old Faithful in Yellowstone National Park in the western U.S. blasts steamy water more than 130 feet (40 m) into the air. Don't get too close—the steam above the vent can top 350°F (177°C).

HOT SPOTS

Yellowstone National Park is a hotbed of hydrothermal—which means "hot water"—activity due to its location atop an enormous volcanic crater. It's home to more than 500 geysers—nearly half the world's total. Iceland is also a prime geyser spot because of its location on the Mid-Atlantic Ridge—a place where two major tectonic plates are slowly drifting apart.

STROKKUR

BUBBLING MUD

Some geothermal features bubble rather than spew. Mud pots form where there is soft rock and less water. Small amounts of hot water, along with gases, erode the surrounding rock to form large pools of bubbling mud. This smelly stew is noisy, too!

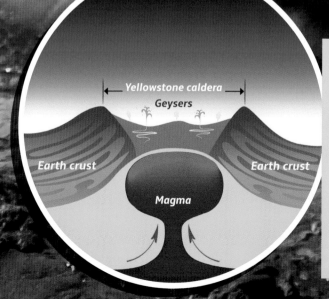

Yellowstone caldera

Geysers

Earth crust

Earth crust

Magma

HOW IT WORKS

A geyser forms from three natural phenomena that are rarely present in the same place. First, there has to be a large supply of underground water. Above the water, a hole or tube must lead to an opening in the surface called a vent. Below the water, fissures and cracks need to be deep and long enough to allow heat from Earth's superhot molten core to reach up to the water. When this heat reaches the water, the liquid turns to steam and ejects upward through the vent, causing a sky-high geyser.

THE SHOCKING SCIENCE
of LIGHTNING

Lightning is so common that you might think scientists have it all figured out. In fact, about 100 lightning bolts streak through the sky every second! But there is one question in particular that continues to puzzle scientists: How does the initial spark form?

A STORMY START

Most thunderstorms happen in summer when the weather is hot. The hot air near the ground rises, and if it hits a cold front, a thundercloud forms. Within this cloud, moisture turns into small bits of ice, which bump into one another, creating an electrical charge. As the thundercloud fills with these electrical charges, positive charges form at the top of the cloud and negative charges form at the bottom. In the world of electricity, opposites attract. Experts believe that when energy surges build up between the negative charges and positive charges, an electric spark discharges—lightning! But scientists don't know for sure, so there's more research to be done.

SEARCHING THE SKIES

Scientists at Los Alamos National Laboratory in New Mexico, U.S.A., are hoping to uncover the mysteries behind lightning. The lab identified a process called fast positive breakdown (FPB), which they think might initiate the lightning flashes typically seen in thunderstorms. The "fast" part of FPB refers to the speed at which this supercharged air—air filled with an accumulation of electric charges—travels. It moves up to 328,083,989 feet (100 million m) per second.

In FPB, the charged air moves downward from a positive to a negative region. This discovery is surprising, because previous studies suggested that the energy moved from the negative to the positive—upward in a cloud—and that is what triggers the lightning flash. This new theory shows that lightning moves in both directions. This idea gets us closer to understanding lightning, but it doesn't provide all the answers.

SEA STRIKES

Meanwhile, scientists at the University of Washington made a related, startling discovery. Over a 10-year period, twice as many lightning strikes occurred over cargo shipping lanes than above the surrounding seas. Why? The researchers say the ships don't *attract* lightning, but they seem to *contribute* to it. Particles of pollution released by the ships' engines float into the clouds. These exhaust particles mix with moisture to create ice crystals, which rub against one another, causing a buildup of electrical charges.

LIGHTING THE WAY

More study has to be done to illuminate the mystery of how lightning starts. Scientists across the world—and in space—are using advanced detection instruments to measure electrical charges, space station experiments, lightning-mapping satellites, and more to solve the mystery. We're getting closer than ever to shining a light on how lightning gets its spark.

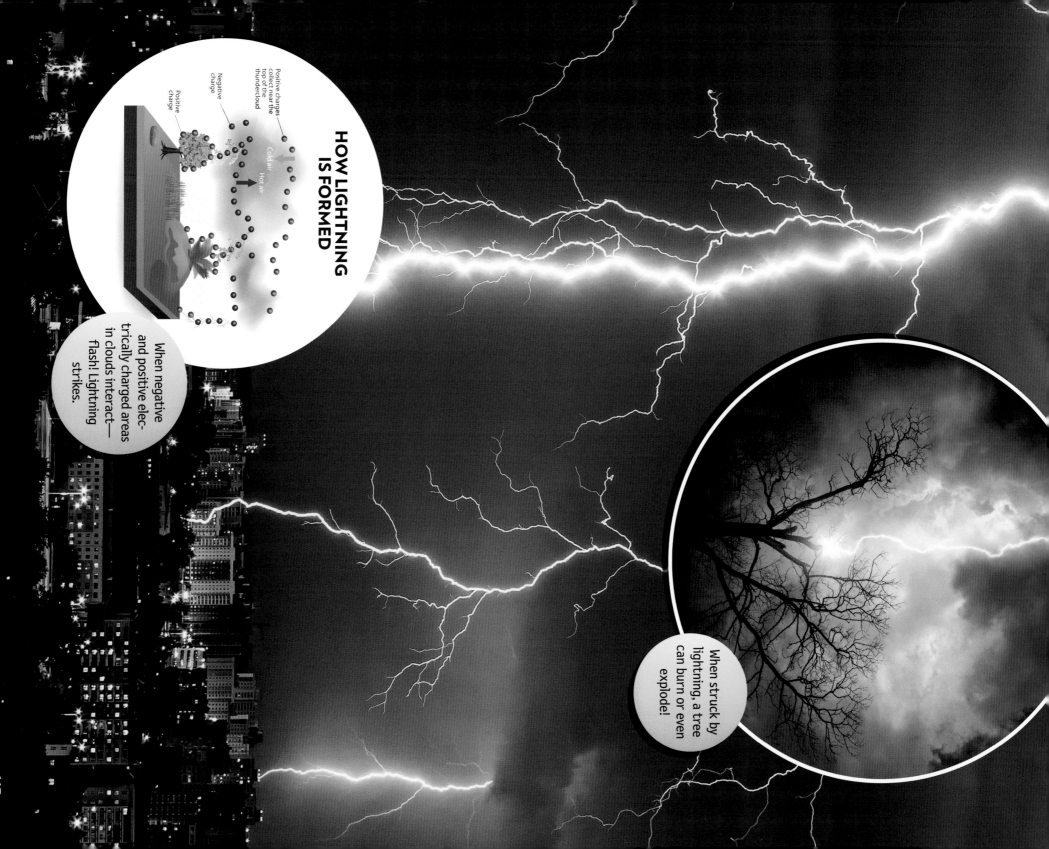

HOW LIGHTNING IS FORMED

Positive charges collect near the top of the thundercloud

Negative charge

Positive charge

Cold air

Hot air

When negative and positive electrically charged areas in clouds interact—flash! Lightning strikes.

When struck by lightning, a tree can burn or even explode!

115

CRAZY COLORS IN NATURE

SPLATTER ART

For a few months every year, Colombia's Caño Cristales River is awash with color—splotches of red, blue, yellow, orange, and green that earned it the nickname "river of five colors." At the root of this phenomenal display is a unique aquatic plant, *Macarenia clavigera*. Rising water levels at the end of the rainy season prompt this plant to change color. Its brilliant red blooms, offset by blue waters and yellow sand, create the kaleidoscope of color.

FROZEN WONDERLAND

Kamchatka Cave, in Russia, sparkles in white and gray. That's because it's an ice cave—a deep tunnel through a glacier, formed by a hot spring. But sometimes the icy interior glows with a dazzling display of blue and violet lights. This colorful change happens when sunlight streams through the cave's thin walls—or tries to. Snow and ice reflect much of the sunlight that reaches their surface, but blue and violet shades get through.

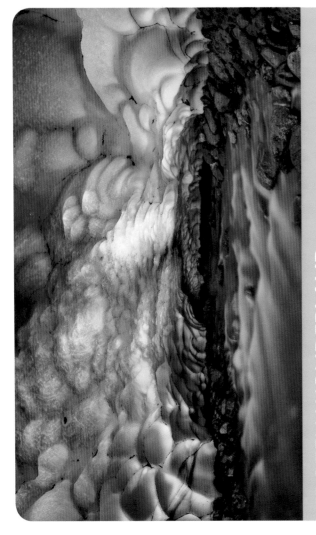

THINK PINK

Have you ever wanted to know what a swimming pool filled with strawberry milkshake might look like? Look no further than Australia's Lake Hillier. This aquatic oddity is a bizarre bubblegum pink! The cause of the lake's crazy color has baffled scientists for years. Experts originally guessed that the culprit might be a type of algae known to make other bodies of water turn different hues. But a recent DNA analysis of its waters revealed Hillier's true secret: high quantities of *Salinibacter ruber*—a red-pigmented bacteria (*ruber* is Latin for "red") that thrives in salt water and makes this lake pretty in pink.

BLUE LAKES, GREEN LEAVES, SLATE-GRAY MOUNTAINS—ALL PRETTY NORMAL SIGHTS. BUT NATURE SOMETIMES PRODUCES SOME IMAGINATIVE AND UNEXPECTED HUES.

STRIPED SLOPES

The Rainbow Mountains of China's Gansu Province are a masterpiece of geological artistry. The candy-colored landforms look like layer cake, but the recipe was millions of years in the making. Red sandstone and minerals were deposited in layers, baked in the sun, and tilted by earthshaking tectonic activity. Millions of years of wind and sand erosion eventually exposed these colorful, curvy cliffs.

SPECTACULAR STEVE

When everyday sky watchers in Canada first noticed a remarkable purple ribbon of light in the night sky, they called it ... Steve. The name might have started as a joke, but the scientists who confirmed the phenomenon's presence officially named it Strong Thermal Emission Velocity Enhancement, and the name stuck. Researchers first thought STEVE was a type of aurora, like the famous northern lights, but experts now say it's actually a new type of celestial phenomenon. To keep track of STEVE, a citizen science project called Aurorasaurus was established, so new sightings can be reported wherever in the world STEVE might shine.

VIBRANT VALLEY

Nestled high in the Himalaya, India's Valley of Flowers National Park is home to more than 600 types of plant life—most of them wildflowers. Many of these species are endemic to the valley, meaning they exist nowhere else on Earth. That's thanks to the park's remote location: in a valley where two mountain ranges meet, creating a microclimate ideal for growing flowers. The valley's setting makes it hard for plants and their seeds to be easily transported out of the valley by wildlife or humans, so many of the flowers there are unique to this location.

The Valley of Flowers is also home to rare and endangered animals, including snow leopards and blue sheep. You can visit this site, but to get there you'll need to trek 10.5 miles (17 km) on foot or ride a pony—no cars are allowed.

LIGHT IT UP!

BIOLUMINESCENT ANIMALS LIGHT UP THE WORLD IN UNIQUE WAYS. SOME SPARKLE TO SEND A MESSAGE, OTHERS TO ILLUMINATE THEIR SURROUNDINGS. For a flashy few, it's a clever means of disguise. Meet some of Earth's most luminous life-forms.

HANDY HEADLAMP

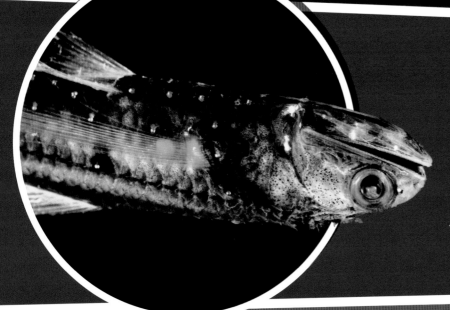

In the deepest ocean waters, there's almost no light from the sun. These nightlike conditions don't bother the lanternfish, which has a number of features to help it survive in ocean depths of up to 3,000 feet (914 m). Extra-large eyes enable it to gather as much light as possible, and tiny organs along its sides, called photophores, light up to announce its presence to potential mates. The light-producing organ in its nose is probably its best survival tool. This built-in head-light shines a spotlight on prey, making the lanternfish an effective deep-sea hunter.

FLASH AND CRASH

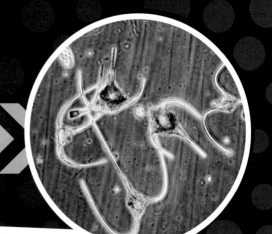

Dinoflagellates (a kind of plankton) have a neat trick. These single-celled algae can't defend themselves from hungry creatures like copepods (tiny crustaceans). Instead, they light up to attract larger predators, which go after their attackers. This defensive maneuver depends on teamwork: Individual dinoflagellates don't produce enough light to lure in defenders. But in large numbers, their combined flashing does the trick.

ALLURING LIGHT

The female black dragonfish has a light-producing barbel (whisker-like growth) dangling from its chin. It uses this fishy beard as bait, bobbling it to attract potential meals. When unsuspecting prey comes within reach, the dragonfish snaps it up in fanglike teeth.

INVISIBILITY CLOAK

Small and soft-bodied, the bobtail squid owes its survival to some helpful hitchhikers—glowing bacteria that live in a pouch on its underbelly. The little squid spends its daylight hours hiding in sand on the seafloor. At night, it emerges to hunt, with a little help from its bacterial buddies. Their glow helps the squid blend in with light from the moon and stars in a form of camouflage called counterillumination. Predators looking up from below can't make out the squid's silhouette. The light also blots out the squid's shadow, so it can sneak up on prey.

FREAKY FUNGI

The jack-o'-lantern mushroom got its spooky name not just for its bright orange color, but also because it emits an eerie glow on autumn nights. Could the freaky light be the work of a ghastly ghost? Not likely. The mushroom's gills glow due to the presence of an enzyme called luciferase. Out of the nearly 100,000 species of fungi on Earth, only about 80 of them can glimmer in the gloom. The light attracts insects that eat the mushroom and help spread its spores through the forest.

There's a saltwater lake where you can **SWIM ALONGSIDE** hundreds of thousands of **golden jellyfish.**

HOW DID THESE OCEAN DWELLERS END UP IN A LAKE?

Tentacled jellyfish might not sound like something you'd find during a dip in a peaceful mountain pool. But on Eil Malk Island in Palau, located in the Pacific Ocean near the Philippines and Indonesia, there are five special salty bodies of water, called marine lakes, filled with these squishy species.

These rare marine lakes formed millions of years ago, when volcanic eruptions created a group of craggy islands. Then, when the Ice Age ended, sea levels rose, flooding the islands' valleys and forming the saltwater lakes. Sea creatures drifted in with the floodwaters and became cut off from the ocean.

The most famous of these bodies of water is Palau's Jellyfish Lake, named for the massive numbers of golden jellyfish that grace its waters. This species is found nowhere else on Earth and can range from the size of a basketball down to about as small as a coffee mug. Their sting is harmless to the humans who swim in their midst.

That's SUPER COOL!

121

ASK AN EXPERT

Glacier ice looks blue. The crystalline structure of the ice scatters blue light while absorbing the other colors of the spectrum.

Do glaciers speak?

THE EXPERT: Dr. Erin Pettit, glaciologist (glacier expert), National Geographic Explorer, and founder of Inspiring Girls Expeditions

CAN YOU TELL US WHAT GLACIERS ARE?

A: Glaciers are massive sheets of moving ice formed from compacted snow; they can form on mountains or on land that's always frozen, such as Antarctica. Glaciers flow over the landscape—sometimes dramatically, but usually any movement is very subtle.

DO GLACIERS MAKE NOISES WHEN THEY MOVE?

A: Big calving events (when chunks break off from a glacier's front edge to form an iceberg) create crashing and sloshing sounds. But the most interesting sound to me is the sound of ice melting. Glacier ice is loud when it melts because it contains pressurized bubbles of air. Millions of tiny air bubbles explode out of the ice and into the water—it sounds like drops of water sizzling in a hot frying pan. This sound can tell us how fast ice is melting: A louder sound means ice is melting faster.

BIG CALVING EVENTS SOUND LOUD! HOW CAN YOU HEAR WHAT'S HAPPENING INSIDE A GLACIER?

A: I lower instruments into glacier caves called moulins—vertical tubes that form from the top of a glacier down. They are hollowed out by water flowing on the glacier in the summer. I use sensors that measure water and temperature changes, and hydrophones (underwater microphones) that help me listen to the glacier. I measure the sounds to understand how the glacier works.

WHAT ARE GLACIERS SAYING WHEN THEY SPEAK?

A: These sounds are the glacier telling me stories. By measuring their tones, frequencies, and volume, I can document the process of ice melting—and foresee changes that can ultimately lead to rising sea levels. Melting glacial ice contributes to sea level rise, which affects ecosystems all over the world. Glaciers have the power to change our landscapes, and by understanding them we can learn a lot about our changing climate.

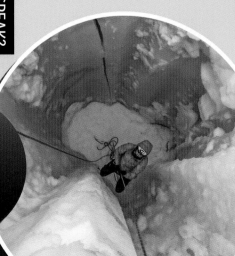

To enter a moulin, experts rappel down from the surface with a rope.

Iguazú Falls, a system of about 275 waterfalls, is in South America's Atlantic Forest. It is 1.7 miles (2.7 km) wide.

SECRETS of TROPICAL

Tropical rainforests cover only about 7 percent of Earth's land, but they're home to an estimated half of all known plant and animal species. Located near the Equator, in areas such as South and Central America, West Africa, and Southeast Asia, this special ecosystem is known for its plentiful precipitation—some tropical rainforests can see up to 400 inches (1,000 cm) of rain per year! In the Amazon, the world's largest rainforest, there are more than 400 mammal species, nearly 800 reptile and amphibian species, and about 1,300 bird species. Add more than 5,000 freshwater fish, tens of thousands of invertebrates, and 40,000 different types of plants, and this tropical paradise is a busy place that works in a unique way.

Up, Down, and All Around

Rainforests are like large, leafy apartment buildings with many residents on each of their four floors (called layers). At the top is the emergent layer. Only the tallest trees reach this level, including kapok trees, which can grow as tall as a 20-story building. Bathed in brilliant sunlight, this sky-high spot is the domain of eagles, butterflies, and some primates.

The most crowded layer is the canopy, which sits in the zone between 75 to 100 feet (23 to 31 m) off the ground. Nine out of 10 rainforest animals live at this level. Thick leaves protect animals from the rain, and a vast network of vines called lianas helps them get around. There are fruits, berries, and flowers for eating and pollinating. Some canopy residents in the Amazon rainforest—howler monkeys and toucans, for example—are homebodies that rarely descend from the trees. Others, including jaguars and many snakes, such as boas, are adventurers that climb, creep,

slither, or fly between the canopy and the lower levels.

The understory (25 to 75 feet, 8 to 23 m) is a shady place—little sunlight filters down to this layer. Plants here are adapted to survive in low-light conditions. Stick insects, spiders, and lizards make their homes in the dimly lit understory.

On the forest floor, shrubs and saplings provide hiding spots for animals. Leaves, seeds, and fruit that fall to the forest floor are broken down by bacteria, insects, and fungi. Anteaters and other ground mammals live here. Agoutis and other small animals build dens in hollow logs or burrow underground. Here, only 2 percent of sunlight reaches the ground—that's about as dark as a bedroom at night with only a dim nightlight glowing.

Rainforests in Danger

These lush locales are being threatened

RAINFORESTS

by climate change, deforestation, and development. The system of the Amazon rainforest works because every factor plays its part: The weather stays rainy, which provides moisture for plants and animals in all the layers of the forest, which provide sources of food and shelter for other plants and animals, and on. When conditions change, everything else in the system is affected. Climate change is increasing the frequency of long-term weather patterns, such as El Niño winds. These swiftly moving cyclical air currents bring dry conditions, which create drought when they happen for long periods of time. Because of this, the rainforest is now less rainy than it used to be.

Conservationists hope that if more people around the globe understand rainforests and how they help our planet, more people will be inspired to protect them and the amazing animals that call these tropical paradises home.

Because of the thick vegetation, it can take more than 10 minutes for a raindrop to fall 100 feet (30 m) to the forest floor!

To many scientists' surprise, a species of tarantula and frog were observed sharing burrows. In this strange relationship, the frog may be protected from other predators; meanwhile the tarantula's eggs are spared—the frog eats ants that would otherwise eat the eggs.

TERRIFIC TREES

Tropical rainforests started growing more than 100 million years ago, and today are home to countless numbers of trees. And trees work hard to keep our planet healthy. Tropical rainforests absorb massive amounts of carbon dioxide, a greenhouse gas that contributes to climate change. The Amazon rainforest alone absorbs one-quarter of the total 2.3 billion tons (2.1 billion t) of carbon dioxide that all forests around the world absorb each year. But logging and deforestation threaten the world's forests, especially the Amazon, which has lost about 17 percent of its trees during the past 50 years. Less forested area means that more greenhouse gases remain trapped in the atmosphere. Humans will need to find a balance to preserve these important forests, which help protect our planet.

OCELOT

SPECTACULAR SPORTS

Around the world, people love to compete. They play sports of all kinds to challenge their bodies, to capture trophies, or just to have fun. They also watch their heroes take part in sports on TV and in packed stadiums and arenas. But there's a lot more to the world of sports than balls and points and touchdowns. Whether you can't wait to hit the ice, jump on the court, take the field, or kick off the game—or you want to discover some cool sports you've never heard of—uncover fascinating facts in this fast-paced chapter.

Competitive
jumping rabbits can

HOP
fences

three times their **height**—
that's like a human athlete
jumping 18 feet (5.5 m) in the air!

HOW DOES
THIS BUNNY HOP
SO HIGH?

Horses and dogs show off their skills by leaping over obstacles on courses, so why not bunnies? To evade their predators, wild rabbits use their powerful back legs to jump long distances and their natural speed to sprint in zigzag patterns. In Sweden in the 1970s, rabbit lovers began training their pet rabbits to jump over high obstacles; then they formed a club to showcase their bunnies' skills. And soon, a hoppin' new international sport was born.

"Rabbit" in Swedish is *kanin*, so the sport there is called *kaninhop*. These long-eared athletes, usually on leashes, run on courses and jump over gates in timed events. Competitions sometimes have agility courses with tunnels, ramps, and bridges for an added challenge. There are rules about the animals' health and care, training dos and don'ts, and competition requirements, too, just like for human sports.

Steph Curry is a master three-point shooter. He jumps higher than average and releases the ball at just the right moment.

SECRETS of
THREE-

A LONG SHOT

Swoosh! The sport of basketball changed forever in 1967 with the founding of the American Basketball Association (ABA). An upstart league challenging the dominance of the National Basketball Association (NBA), it was looking for something new and fresh to grab fans' attention. The ABA decided to add a radical new way of scoring: the three-point shot. If a basket was made from outside an arc drawn around the basket area on each end of the court, the shooter's team got three points

instead of only two. It turned out to be popular with fans. The ABA joined with the NBA in 1976, and in 1979, the NBA introduced the spectacular shot. It went international in 1984, and college hoops followed suit in 1987. Scoring shot up as a result, and basketball became faster and more exciting for fans.

Though it's a harder shot to make than a layup, which earns two points, the benefit of earning that additional point is often worth taking the chance. Adding a three-point line also forced

defenders to move away from the basket to guard shooters beyond that line. By making players spread out, the game began to move faster and scores began to rise.

There's a reason why making a three-pointer is a pro move: Here's how the best shooters "drain treys" (make threes).

Set Up
The rules are clear: Both of a player's feet must be fully behind the entire three-point line before they shoot.

POINTERS

If even a toe is touching the line, the shot is worth only two points. Knowing where the line is, of course, is the first step: The distance between three-point line and the basket varies, depending on which league is playing.

Once a player has the ball, they have to set their feet. Players want to be balanced and steady before the shot, and that starts with setting up a stable base. Most shooters want to have both feet pointed at the basket, with the foot opposite the shooting hand a few inches behind the other one.

Launch Angle

To make a three-pointer, basketball players have to think like scientists! Without physics, three-point shots would be impossible. A player's body generates force to push the ball toward the hoop. How much force? Enough to make it there, of course, but not so much that it bounces hard off the rim or backboard. So how do Stephen Curry or Breanna Stewart drain treys? It's not magic. It's practice. The best way to figure out how much force you need is to shoot ... a lot!

But what goes up must come down. The angle at which the ball makes the flight is part of the shot's success. As the shooter reaches the top of their jump, they release the ball from over (and slightly in front of) their head. The ball should leave the hands at an angle between 33 and 45 degrees. Now, most teams won't let a shooter stop and get out a protractor to measure this angle during play, so the only way to get it right is to practice until launching the ball at the correct angle feels natural.

Ray Allen entered the Hall of Fame in 2018 with 2,973 three-point shots—the current NBA record!

Launching the ball from above the head is crucial to draining treys.

HALFCOURT LINE

BACKBOARD

23.75 ft (7.2 m)
22.15 ft (6.8 m)
20.75 ft (6.3 m)

By the Numbers
Three-point line distances from the top of the arc to the middle of the basket

- NBA
- FIBA, WNBA, & NCAA MEN
- NCAA WOMEN

OLYMPIC LASTS—AND FIRSTS!

GYMNASTICS, SWIMMING, SKIING, TRACK AND FIELD—YOU'VE PROBABLY WATCHED THESE WELL-KNOWN OLYMPIC EVENTS. OLYMPIC ORGANIZERS NEED TO KEEP THE GAMES FRESH, SO THEY ARE ALWAYS EVALUATING THE SPORTS ON THEIR ROSTER. CHECK OUT THESE OTHER EPIC OLYMPIC SPORTS TO SEE WHICH CUTTING-EDGE COMPETITIONS HAVE MADE THE CUT.

TUG-OF-WAR

All together now ... PULL! Whether pulling at a toy with your dog or battling your pals on the playground, tug-of-war takes tons of muscle. Believe it or not, this field-day favorite was once a crowd-pleaser at the Olympics. Introduced in 1900, eight-man teams tugged and pulled on each end of a thick rope, and tried to drag the other team at least six feet (2 m). If no one succeeded, the judges declared five minutes of overtime. After that, the team who had pulled farthest won. But the sport didn't last long: tug-of-war made its last stand at the 1920 Olympics.

SKIJORING

"Giddy-up" may not be something you hear often in ski races, but when you're skijoring, it might come in handy. In this fast-moving winter sport, skiers are pulled by horses! It made its only Olympic appearance in 1928 in St. Moritz, Switzerland, where local hero Rudolf Wettstein (and his horse) finished first. Skijoring never made another Olympic appearance, but that doesn't mean you can't still saddle up. The sport is still played today in Scandinavia and other snowy places.

CROQUET

It's a game enjoyed by royalty and regular residents, on sunny lawns and even the snowy South Pole—croquet! The game originated in 14th-century France, and today it is played on grass, where a ball is hit through a series of wickets (half-hoops) with a long-handled mallet. While this sport may remind you of a friendly backyard barbecue, competitive croquet was actually part of the 1900 Paris Summer Olympics. At the time, it was popular in England and France, though apparently not a big hit on the world stage—the 1900 games were croquet's first and last appearance. But it was one of the first Olympic sports that allowed women to participate, kicking off a century of strides forward for women in the games.

SKATEBOARDING

Skaters shredding in both park and street are new to the Olympic Games. In park events, skaters ride on, over, around, and above a series of obstacles in a setting similar to a drained pool. In street events, the course is built to resemble a cityscape, with rails, curbs, jumps, and flat areas to do tricks.

CLIMBING

In sport climbing, athletes scale textured walls dotted with handholds used to pull themselves up by their hands and push off with their feet. In 2016, the best climbers in the world learned they would be competing in the next Summer Olympics. The speed event is basically "race you to the top!" In bouldering, climbers have to find a fast way through a tricky set of holds. And in lead climbing, competitors get six minutes to get as far as they can up a wall that is 49.2 feet (15 m) tall.

SURFING

"Hang ten for gold" was the cry from the water as surfers were told this sport would be making its Olympic debut. Competitors in surfing are judged by how many tricks they do in each heat, along with how well they do them. The tricky part for fans? Since ocean waves are required to hold the competition, the event can only happen when the waves at Summer Games are big enough. That means lots of waiting for just the right moment. It's a good thing surfers are so chill!

FLY AWAY!

Before there were airplanes and helicopters, people took to the skies in hot-air balloons.

Today, hot-air ballooning is a sport and an adventure. Discover how balloons take off and stay up, how they fly and land, and more. There's nowhere to go from here but up!

NO STAMP REQUIRED

The balloon skin itself is called an envelope, and is made of nylon. Most balloons are, well ...balloon-shaped, like a long teardrop. But nylon is very flexible, and people are very creative. So balloons come in just about every shape you can think of—Santas, carrots, owls, soda cans, cartoon characters, castles, cars, and yes, even underwear!

A DIFFERENT KIND OF BREEZY

In 1785, a pair of fliers wanted to be the first to balloon across the English Channel. The two pilots were, um, not very good at ballooning. They battled gravity all the way across and had to jettison (toss out) just about everything except themselves. One of the men even tossed his pants overboard. Hey, every ounce counts.

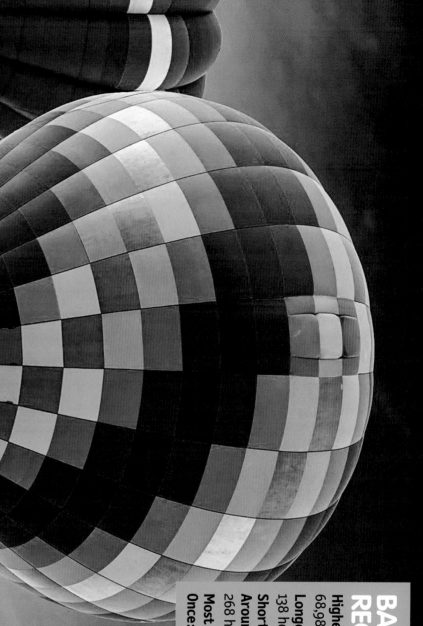

FULL OF HOT AIR

Air is made of molecules, which move around faster when they're warm, creating more space between them. So when balloons are filled with air heated by a flame, that air weighs less than the cooler air outside the balloon. The hot air inside the balloon rises, lifting the balloon with it.

STANDING ROOM ONLY

Pilot and passengers stand in a wicker basket that hangs from the bottom of the envelope. Wicker's flexibility helps cushion the basket when it comes time to land.

A LOFTY ADVENTURE

There's no steering wheel in a balloon, so the wind is in charge of its flight path. For a safe journey, balloonists need a clear sky and a day without too much wind. Once aloft, the pilot can control only whether the craft goes up or down—no turns! To descend, the pilot releases the hot air by pulling on a cord that opens a flap on the crown (top) of the balloon. As the hot air exits, colder air rushes in, making the balloon slowly float down to the ground.

BALLOONING RECORDS

Highest Flight:
68,986 feet (21,027 m)

Longest Flight (Time):
138 hours and 45 minutes

Shortest Time for an Around-the-World Flight:
268 hours, 20 minutes

Most Balloons Aloft at Once: 433

Germany's goalkeeper Manuel Neuer later confided that Lampard's famous "no goal" was good.

136

MAKING THE RIGHT CALL

With a powerful kick, England's star striker, Frank Lampard, ripped a shot at the German goal. The soccer ball smacked into the crossbar and bounced down. Millions of fans watching on TV and in the stands saw a goal. The English players were convinced they had seen one, too. But two people didn't: the referees. Even though video clearly showed that the ball went over the goal line, no goal was awarded. The shocking controversy at the 2010 World Cup changed the sport of soccer forever.

Sports officials keep games safe and fair, and have to make instant decisions in fast-paced environments. Referees decide whether points are scored—or not; and whether players are penalized for errors—or not. And while they are nearly always right, they sometimes make mistakes.

Officials can now rely on cameras, instant replay, and digital tools to help them make the right call. But the modern sporting world faces a big question: Are these high-tech tools actually making sports better?

INSTANT ANSWERS

After Lampard's "no goal," soccer had a problem to fix. After that World Cup, goal-line camera technology was added to the sport. Several cameras now watch the line. If a ball crosses it, a signal is sent to a device on the referee's wrist. Additional tech was added with the Video Assistant Referee (VAR), which lets referees review plays during a game. VAR combines cameras with an off-field official watching TV monitors to help referees review other types of calls, such as whether a player hit the ball with a hand or arm. The on-field official also gets an alert when the VAR official spots a possible foul. The on-field ref then looks at replays on a field-side TV screen to make the final call. This system is working well so far.

SHARPER EYES

In tennis, spotting whether a ball was in or out as it rocketed across the court at more than 120 miles an hour (193 km/h) has always been a crucial role of officiating. It was a hard job and often led to arguments. In 2001, the Hawk-Eye system was added to the top televised tournaments. Ten cameras eyeball every line on the court. Players or officials can ask to look at the camera results to confirm that a ball was correctly called in or out. The results are instantly seen by players and officials on the court and fans on TV.

Baseball umpires already use replays to decide tag plays at bases. But what about balls and strikes? They are the heart of the game, and a single umpire decides whether a pitch is in or out of the strike zone. The rules say the zone is armpits to knees, but umpires' standards vary a lot. On TV, fans can see graphics that show how a pitch crossed the plate. Umps and players on the field in real time can't.

In 2019, the Atlantic League in the minor leagues experimented with in-game strike-zone tech called TrackMan, which relies on Doppler radar to show where a ball crossed home plate. (Yes, the tech used to track weather systems can also track a moving baseball!) This test-drive may lead to a trial run in the majors.

REFS OF THE FUTURE

While technology makes officials' decisions more accurate, there are downsides. Sports struggle with long games. In baseball, for example, games often take three or more hours. Reviewing more and more plays with tech could slow games down even more. The bottom line is, everyone wants to see the right calls made ... even if we need help from tech.

The friction of the metal blade melts a thin layer of ice, creating water over which the blades can glide.

What is the **key** to **skating** like a pro?

THE EXPERT: Barb Underhill, former Olympian and world champion pairs figure skater with partner Paul Martini; National Hockey League coach; co-owner of Ontario Hockey League team Guelph Storm

Figure skaters use the toe pick—sawlike teeth at the front of the skate blade—to launch into spins and jumps.

Q: WHAT ARE THE BASICS OF ICE-SKATING?

A: To skate, you have to be able to pick your feet up one at a time. To do that, your feet have to be underneath your center of gravity. When you're balanced on one blade, it's easier to bend your joints (hip, knee, and ankle) to create pressure on the blade that's on the ice. That pressure turns into force, and that force helps you move forward.

Center your weight over one blade, say the left foot. Then, line up your nose over your left knee as you glide on that skate. Keeping your upper body stable, lean your weight into the ice over the left skate as you step forward with the right foot, and shift your weight onto the right skate. Like walking, you shift your weight from foot to foot—but put your feet are pushing out at a 45-degree angle to the ice instead of moving in a straight line.

Q: HOW DO PROS MAKE AWESOME ICE-SPRAYING STOPS?

A: They have had a lot of practice, of course! It's very hard to stop on both feet. In ice hockey, a stop is basically the start of the next move, so hockey players transfer their weight rapidly from the stopping skate to the other skate to get moving again quickly. One foot does the main stopping (by pushing the inner skate edge hard into the ice) while the other starts the next move. For example, if a pro is turning to the right, they lean that way with their body and the left skate does the work of digging in to start the turn; their right skate is already planting on the ice to accelerate out of the turn.

Q: HOW ARE ICE HOCKEY AND FIGURE SKATING DIFFERENT?

A: There are a lot of differences in the sports, of course, but a key difference is the type of skate used. Both hockey and figure skates have a metal blade attached to the bottom of a boot. And on both types of skates, the blades have a slight hollow on the bottom that creates two sharp edges. Figure skates have a toe pick (the serrated part at the front of the blade) that skaters use to dig into the ice to launch into jumps, plus a high boot with a heel and blades that are longer than the boot. Hockey skate blades are curved at both ends, are the same length as the boot, and are attached a bit differently. Hockey players generally don't jump—they use their edges for fast, sharp turns.

Q: IS THERE A SECRET TO WHY THE PROS ARE ABLE TO SKATE WAY BETTER THAN WE CAN?

A: Cross-training! They do strength training for their legs and core. Mobility is really important for skaters, and many do yoga to stay flexible. Too much muscle won't make you skate better if you can't move your joints well. Today's pros make sure to balance strength and flexibility and range of motion. If you're too stiff, you won't be a good skater. Like everything in skating, balance is the key.

FIGURE SKATE

HOCKEY SKATE

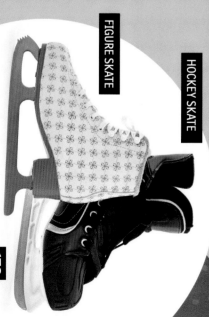

139

Long-distance **runners** can

SHRINK

up to half an inch (1.3 cm) in height while **running a race.**

HOW CAN RUNNING MAKE YOU SHORTER?

Marathon runners put one foot in front of the other to race mile after mile—26.2 miles (42.2 km) to be exact. These elite runners aren't just getting a workout, they're actually getting a little bit shorter. What's going on to make this happen? The spinal column in the back is made up of a series of bones called vertebrae that are separated by soft tissue called disks.

As a long-distance runner pounds out the miles, these disks are compressed over and over again with every step. The force of this compression squashes the disks down. The disks are about 70 percent water, and a little bit leaks out into the surrounding tissue, making the disks smaller. As a result, the vertebrae between the disks move closer together, shortening the spinal column. So, runners shrink!

But don't throw away your running shoes. Experts point out that it's only a temporary change. After rehydrating and some rest, runners are back to their usual height. If that didn't happen, a marathon champion like Paula Radcliffe might be only three feet tall (1 m) by now!

However, it's not just speedy runners who shrink: This process is something that happens to everyone every day, just from walking around. Don't become a couch potato yet, though—the height change from everyday activity is so small that most of us don't even notice it. When we sleep, our spinal column returns to normal.

The Ultimate
HOME RUN

Here's the pitch—the home run is the biggest hit in baseball. It's a perfect blend of skill, timing, and physics.

A hitter turns a baseball into a missile bound for the bleachers, helping the team toward victory. Here's a coach's clinic of home run secrets.

OUTTA THE PARK

Home runs are on the rise in baseball. In 2019, the Minnesota Twins set a new single-season record by smacking 307 homers. In the past few seasons, Major League Baseball (MLB) teams have hit more of them than ever. There are more teams now (30) than in the past, but even by per-team averages, homers are up. Between 2015 and 2019, the per-game average for a team increased from 1.01 homers to 1.40 homers during the regular season. In 1998, the first year with 30 teams, it was 1.04. In 1960, when MLB still had 16 teams, the average was .86— not even one per game.

YARDWORK!

It's called a home run because after hitting the ball, players run around the diamond and back to home base, scoring for their team. But the home run has many awesome nicknames, including dinger, tater, long ball, *cuadrangular* (Spanish), and yardwork.

Sweet Spot
For maximum power, a batter tries to hit the ball on the sweet spot—just a couple of inches from the fat end of the bat.

142

BATTER UP!

A batter needs to perfectly position the body—from the head to the feet—to get the most power. And power is exactly what you need to hit a homer.

Swing Science
Batters aim for a 25- to 30-degree launch angle to hit a homer. The launch angle compares the direction the bat is moving to the level field.

Swing Path
Today's batters swing UP at the ball instead of on a flat plane.

More Power
A player uses the back foot to push toward the ball.

Eyes
The batter keeps their head down and eyes aimed at where the bat meets the ball.

Arms
A player keeps both arms extended during the swing.

Power
By twisting the torso forcefully, a batter generates power.

143

WORLD OF WACKY SPORTS

LOOKING FOR A NEW SPORT THAT'S OFFBEAT, UNUSUAL, OR JUST PLAIN WACKY? THERE ARE SURPRISING SPORTS TO BE FOUND ALL OVER THE WORLD. HERE SOME AWESOME WAY-OUT ATHLETICS TO TRY OUT.

A LEG UP

The annual Shin Kicking World Championships are held in Gloucester, Great Britain. The event is part of the Cotswold Olimpicks, which has been around since the early 1600s. Shin kicking involves kicking someone else's shins while they try to kick yours. There are rules about how you can hold your opponent, what types of shoes you can wear, and what kind of padding you can put in your pant leg—straw. A referee called a Stickler declares a winner based on who falls to the ground most often.

DON'T FALL IN!

How do you get across a water-filled canal if there isn't a bridge? For centuries in the Netherlands, farmers working in the fields used a wooden pole to launch themselves to the other side. Then extreme sports lovers took it one step farther—or higher! In *fierljeppen*, which translates to "far-leaping," athletes each must jump onto a very tall pole made from high-tech materials and start climbing as the pole falls toward the other side of a body of water. Whoever lands the farthest from the jumping-off point (and doesn't get wet) is the winner.

HANDLE WITH CARE

Believe it or not, egg tossing is an official sport! The town of Swaton, Great Britain, has hosted the World Egg Throwing Federation's annual world championship since 2005. There are multiple ways to compete, including egg tossing, team relay races, and a smashing game in which two players take turns choosing from six eggs—one of which is raw—and squishing them against their faces. The loser gets a face full of eggy goo. And that's no yolk ... um, joke!

144

NO SKATES ALLOWED

The playing surface in underwater hockey may not be frozen, but the inspiration for the game play and rules definitely comes from ice hockey. Players use one-foot (0.3-m)-long sticks to smack a heavy puck along the bottom of a swimming pool and into their opponents' goal. The tricky part? They have to hold their breath while playing, surfacing as needed to breathe. Six swimmers play for each team, and they can wear flippers, gloves, a mask, and a snorkel.

DOUBLE TROUBLE

Chess requires enormous concentration. Players need to keep thousands of possible moves in their mind and outthink their opponents. So now imagine playing chess while occasionally dodging punches. That's chess boxing. Competitors alternate three-minute rounds of playing chess and boxing. In an official match, there are six rounds of chess and five of boxing. To win, you only need to be best in one of the two competitions: checkmate your opponent in chess or knock him or her out while boxing.

CATCHING AIR

The first things you might notice about this game are the five-foot (1.5 m)-high net, the small ball, and the players on a court. Is it tennis? No. The players don't have rackets. Volleyball? It's not that either. It's sepak takraw, which translates to "kick ball," because the players use their feet to hit the ball. Like soccer, there are no hands allowed. This dynamic, fast-moving game originated in Southeast Asia. Talented players leap so high that they can spike the ball with their feet, hitting it while it's above their head as they flip and fly around.

8

MONEY DECODED

Have a keen eye for cash? We use it every day, but there are many marvelous money mysteries hidden in plain sight. We may think of money as a way to pay for things we want and need. But it's so much more than that! It can also cover a world of weird excess—from pampering our pooches in preposterous ways to buying a nickel for more than $4 million! Read on to learn about the hidden secrets on a dollar bill, extravagant eggs that are definitely not for breakfast, a famous hill of gold, and much, much more.

SPECTACULAR SPENDING SPREES

MONEY CAN'T BUY HAPPINESS, BUT IT CAN BUY SOME EXTREME EXTRAVAGANCES. FROM AMAZING APPAREL—ANTIQUE UNDIES?—TO RARE CURRENCY, CHECK OUT THESE WILD WAYS TO SPEND A FORTUNE.

THE WHEEL DEAL

It's no secret that car buffs will spend big when it comes to having the coolest, most exclusive ride. Powerful motors, sleek designs, and cool hubcaps are just the beginning. There are leather seats that heat up and cool down, and give back massages; magnificent music systems; and multiple TVs to amp up the entertainment element. Add a built-in espresso maker for a quick pick-me-up, a portable shower for surfers and campers on the go, or colorful light displays just for fun, and you can have a rad ride unlike any other. Special paint colors—from perfect pink to stunning silver to all-over chrome—add a personal touch. But for maximum glam, think all-over bling like this awesome auto covered with 300,000 sparkly crystals. Priced at nearly $1,000,000, it's a bedazzled beauty!

GALAXY QUEST

The first tourist to visit the International Space Station (ISS) paid $20 million for an eight-day trip in 2001. That guy got a deal. In 2008, Richard Garriott used $30 million of the money he had made creating video games to fly to the ISS. Worried about your wallet? Good news, future space tourists: Prices won't be quite as astronomical. Some private companies are taking orders for short space rides. The cost? A mere $200,000!

THE FOUR-MILLION-DOLLAR NICKEL

How can five cents be worth more than $4 million? Enter the incredibly rare United States 1913 Liberty Head nickel. Only five of these nickels were ever made. Three are part of private collections, and the other two are in museums, including the Smithsonian Institution. Coin collecting, also called numismatics, can be an expensive habit, and collectors usually pay much more than face value for sought-after change. A U.S. silver dollar from 1794 once sold for $10 million. Only the rarest coins fetch that much, but check your change ... you never know what might turn up.

OVERPAYING FOR UNDERWEAR

In 2016, a pair of Queen Victoria's under-wear sold at an antique clothing auction for 16,250 British pounds—about $20,000 U.S. dollars! Described as "fine linen drawers with draw-string waist," the royal undies were embroidered with the queen's insignia and date to the late 1800s.

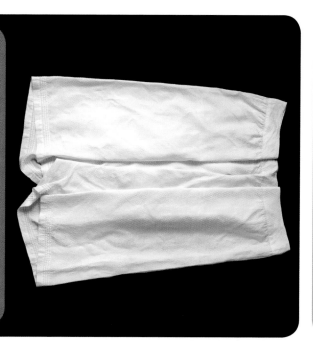

A MELON WORTH MILLIONS

An 1890 $1,000 U.S. treasury note—nicknamed the Grand Watermelon because the zeros on one side resemble the giant fruit—is one of the most precious pieces of paper in existence. The Grand Watermelon was auctioned in 2014 for $3.29 million, the most ever paid for a single piece of U.S. paper money. Only a few dozen of these bills are known to exist, most in museums.

PHENOMENAL PHONES

Whether it's a fun phone case, cool keychain, or awesome accessories, people love blinged-out cell phones. This bejeweled beauty sports 439 rubies, two emeralds, and two large diamonds—and cost about $333,000. Some people take things even further. A phone with more than 500 diamonds set around its edge and a case made of rose gold cost the owner a whopping $8 million. And a royal princess with a preference for pink had her pure gold cell phone set with an enormous pink diamond on the back and smaller jewels around the screen. The cost? More than $48 million! Is there an app for that?

People in the United States
spend $72 billion on their
PETS each year.

That's SUPER COOL!

GIVING PETS THE VERY BEST

All pets need everyday care like food, toys, and trips to the vet. But $72 billion doesn't come from kibble alone. More and more Americans are spending a little extra on Fido. And when it comes to special occasions, some people love to spoil their animal friends. Some go to extremes and buy luxury items and services, including extravagant kitty condos, pet fitness trainers, swim coaches, jewel-encrusted leashes, and even a doghouse with a working shower! But while there are certainly owners who drop some serious dough for their best animal buds, one of the fastest-growing spending categories might surprise you—pet costumes. More than 30 million Americans buy Halloween costumes for their animals. Every year on Halloween, they dress their pooch as a pumpkin and their cat as a cupcake and other fun costumes. Owners can even show them off at the many pet Halloween events that take place around the country. One costume parade in New York City attracts about 25,000 people each year! Turns out pet dress-up is expensive: Americans spent $480 million on pet costumes alone in 2018.

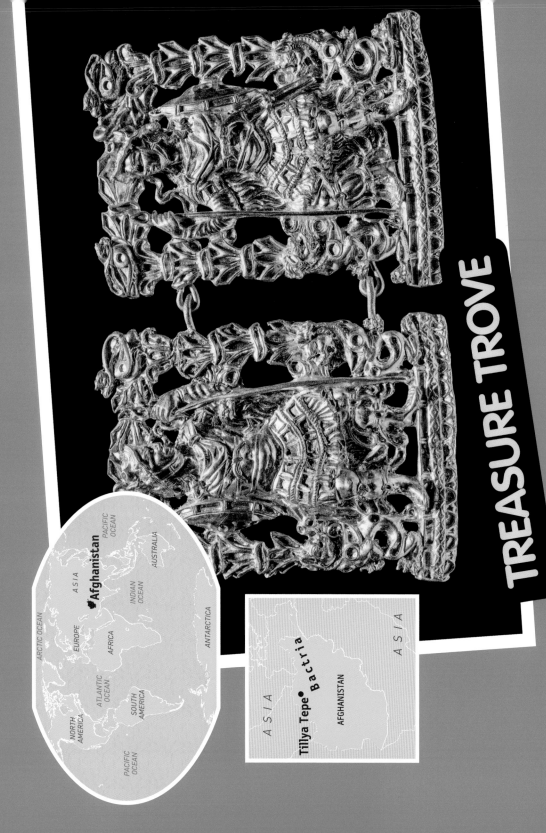

SECRETS of AFGHANISTAN'S

When an archaeologist digging in Afghanistan came across a hidden tomb in 1978, he made an astonishing discovery. Golden belts, rings and bracelets of jade, earrings, bowls, and many, many gold coins were revealed for the first time in nearly 2,000 years. This amazing treasure trove came to be called the Bactrian Hoard at Tillya Tepe, which means "golden hill." The find lived up to its name: In all, there were more than 20,000 pieces of gold weighing a total of 48.5 pounds (22 kg)! Even more important than the wealth of the hoard, finding these riches paved the way for scientists and historians to learn about the people and cultures who buried the treasures with their dead.

Buried Treasure

The tombs of six people—their bodies adorned with masses of gold

jewelry—were unearthed in a remote mountain area at a crossroads of ancient cultures. The find was stunning. The gold buried there came from some of the richest places on Earth at the time: an Indian necklace featuring golden dragons decorated with turquoise and garnets, a golden-handled dagger decorated with a snarling bear, and precious carvings of animals and mythical creatures. Gleaming gold coins from Rome, Greece, India, and Parthia were discovered clutched in the hands of the people buried in the tombs.

As archaeologists studied the artifacts, their questions mounted. How did treasures from as far away as China end up in the Tillya Tepe tombs? And who were these wealthy dead people?

Shopping Trips

When the ancients wanted new furniture or a piece of jewelry, they had

to do quite a bit more than click the "buy" button. Large groups of people carried things—sometimes on camels—that were grown and made in one country to other lands. These journeys followed trade routes dotted with stops along the way called trading posts, where goods were exchanged and sold for things needed back home. The ancient region of Bactria, where Tillya Tepe was located, spread across several modern-day nations, including Afghanistan, Uzbekistan, and Tajikistan. It was part of the Silk Road, a trading route that connected China to regions in the West. Traders would travel through India, the Middle East, Egypt, and then to the Mediterranean ports. Because of these early trade routes, coins, jewels, and other goods ended up in far-flung places like Tillya Tepe.

In the same way that ancient Egyptians filled the pyramids with

ANCIENT ARTIFACTS

riches, the tomb builders at Tillya Tepe placed a variety of objects that might be needed during the afterlife into these tombs—not only the jewelry and gold, but also pottery and tools. Also like the Egyptians, not just anyone would have been buried in such lavish fashion. The dead found there were likely wealthy, important people of their time—possibly even royalty.

Learning From the Past

By finding treasures from so many different places, archaeologists were able to compare the ways different societies honored and buried their dead. They also looked at how the styles and decorations of the objects were similar or different. By seeing what the cultures had left behind, modern scientists learned what those societies valued, and discovered more about how they had lived.

HIDDEN AND FOUND AGAIN

After its discovery, the Bactrian Hoard was housed at the National Museum of Afghanistan, where all people could learn from its rich history. Soon after the discovery, war ravaged Afghanistan. The museum was damaged, and no one knew whether the gold treasures had survived. When peace returned to the region, the mystery of its survival was revealed. In a top-secret plan, museum and government officials had stashed the hoard in a bank basement, where the ancient artifacts remained out of sight. When it was safe, the treasure was returned to the museum.

A worldwide museum tour followed, showing off more than 200 of the treasures unearthed at Tillya Tepe's golden hill. A delicate golden crown was the centerpiece of the exhibit. After more than 2,000 years underground, the crown gleamed in the light once more, a tribute to the brave people who saved it.

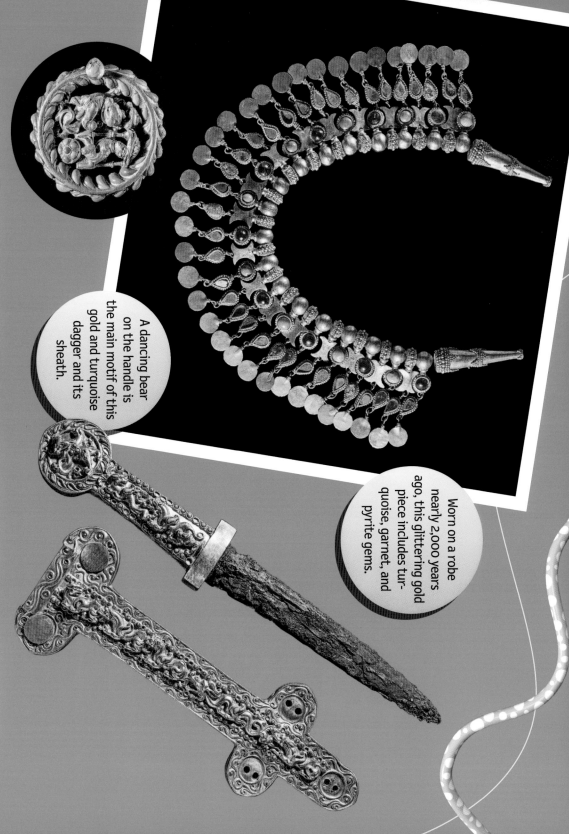

A dancing bear on the handle is the main motif of this gold and turquoise dagger and its sheath.

Worn on a robe nearly 2,000 years ago, this glittering gold piece includes turquoise, garnet, and pyrite gems.

153

EXPENSIVE EGG ENIGMA

It's a mystery that has taken twists and turns over the years—and it's all about eggs. In 1885, Czar Alexander III Romanov, who reigned over Russia, Poland, and Finland, ordered Peter Carl Fabergé, the most famous jewelrymaker in the world, to design and build 10 jewel-encrusted golden Easter eggs. When Alexander died, his son Czar Nicholas II Romanov ordered 40 more. The final egg was completed in 1916. Each of these Fabergé eggs is unique. Some are covered with jewels, while others are hollow and include miniature treasures. Following the Russian Revolution, which ended Romanov rule in 1918, the famous eggs were claimed by the new U.S.S.R. government. But all the eggs were not in one basket.

OPULENT OVALS

Fabergé eggs have been bought and sold around the world—sometimes for only hundreds of dollars, and then, as their value ascended, for much more. In 2004, nine eggs were sold for a total of $100 million—about $11 million each. Why so much? Besides their beauty, these eggs are super rare. The jeweler Fabergé died soon after he left Russia in 1918, so no more true Fabergé eggs were ever made.

Plus, the eggs' connection to a dynasty that ended dramatically make them must-haves for rich collectors.

COUNTING THE COLLECTION

The Fabergé eggs that were recovered in 1918 were held by the new Soviet government and hidden in Moscow vaults. By the 1930s, the U.S.S.R. had sold some of the eggs to raise money. Ten of the sold eggs ended up in the hands of a collector in the United States.

In addition to these 10, another 10 remain in Russia inside the Kremlin (the seat of government), and 10 are in St. Petersburg, Russia, in the Fabergé Museum. Others are kept in museums around the world, including the United States, Switzerland, Germany, and Qatar. Queen Elizabeth II of the United Kingdom personally owns three of the amazing Fabergé eggs.

MISSING EGGS

Where were the rest of the eggs? There was no record of their whereabouts—that is, until 2010. That year, a man found a golden egg at a flea market in the U.S. He bought it for $13,302, figuring the gold was worth that much by weight. He got a big surprise when he tracked down the meaning of words written on the egg and discovered it was one of the missing eight. In 2015, he sold what he now knew to be Fabergé's Third Imperial Easter Egg for $33 million.

KEEP AN EYE OUT

There are still seven ovals to be found, so people will keep searching until all have been recovered. Treasure hunters study old newspapers, diaries, and other media for clues. The greatest Easter egg hunt of all time continues!

The Clover Leaf Egg is too delicate to travel with Fabergé exhibitions. It has never left Russia.

Pearls set with diamonds mimic the shape of the lily of the valley, Empress Alexandra's favorite flower.

The "surprise" in the Coronation egg is a mini carriage not even four inches (10 cm) long. The little carriage alone took more than a year to design.

RICH ROYAL REGALIA

SHINY, SPARKLY, GOLDEN, AND GLOWING ... AND THEIR WORTH? Priceless! Kings, queens, and other royal family members wear these wondrous sets of jewels for ceremonies and special occasions. Here's an inside look at some of the most brilliant baubles from around the world.

TERRIFIC TIARAS

These high-priced headpieces are usually reserved for queens and princesses. Called tiaras, they are similar to hair bands—except they're encrusted with dazzling decorations, including diamonds, emeralds, and more. The royal family of Norway boasts an impressive collection of 17 tiaras, some worn exclusively by Queen Sonja, who has ruled since 1991. While most of the tiaras have a long history, the queen received a modern one to celebrate her 60th birthday. Made of gold with a single diamond, it can be customized, depending on the queen's mood or outfit, to add a piece of gold, green tourmaline, or topaz.

GOLDEN APPLE

Next to the royal crown inside a vault protected by seven locks is a very special apple. But this is not a crisp Red Delicious or Granny Smith. The Royal Apple is part of the crown jewels of the kingdom of Bohemia (now a part of the Czech Republic). Made of 18-karat gold and topped with a jewel-encrusted golden cross, this orb is ornamented with precious pearls and gemstones, including blue sapphires and red spinels. The Royal Apple is displayed with a massive crown and a wand-like ceremonial scepter.

GLORIOUS GOLD

West Africa has vast natural resources of gold—the precious metal treasured around the world. In Ghana, the Akan people have been expert goldsmiths for centuries, turning out medals, sculptures, jewelry, and other beautiful items. Their royal chiefs wear gold from head to toe—literally!—from gold-adorned headdresses to regal rings and brilliant bracelets to gold leaf–encrusted sandals.

FASHION PLATE

During the Middle Ages, full-body armor was heavy duty. Made primarily of steel plates, these protective suits weighed up to 100 pounds (45 kg). And when worn by kings and other members of the court, they were fancy as well as fierce. Created by the finest artists and craftsmen, they were emblazoned with gold, silver, pearls, and gemstones. This suit, made in 1586 for an English earl who was a favorite of Queen Elizabeth I, was lavishly decorated: The steel was tinted and covered with elaborate designs, and it was encrusted with glittering gold.

HEFTY HEADGEAR

Leading a country is a heavy responsibility—especially in Thailand, where the Great Crown of Victory weighs in at just over 15 pounds (7 kg). That's like wearing four or five dictionaries! But this heavy headpiece isn't the only oversize item this royal leader receives. After his coronation, the king of Thailand is presented with the Royal Nine-Tiered Umbrella, made of silk trimmed with gold. This tall topper isn't for rainy days—it towers over the king's throne and represents his responsibility to protect the people.

High-powered

COIN
PRESSES

stamp designs
onto blanks,
forcefully hitting
both sides at once.

Each press can mint
more than
700
coins in a minute.

That's SUPER COOL!

158

KA-CHING!

In 1793, the U.S. minted its first coins—just 11,793 pennies. Today, there are more than 2.2 billion pennies in circulation, along with enough nickels, dimes, and other denominations to top $3.8 billion. Maintaining a steady supply of circulating coinage keeps the hydraulic presses humming at the U.S. Mint in Philadelphia, Pennsylvania. But the Mint has another mission, too. A team of medallic artists design numismatic and bullion products—that's coins for collectors and investors. New designs, one for each side of each special coin, are drawn, or drafted, in 2D. If approved for production, a 3D model is then sculpted in clay, on a computer, or with a combination of these. This model is used to create tooling for coin manufacture. U.S. collectors' coin designs include sets that honor Mark Twain, the national parks, and the Apollo 11 space program. Can you guess what it takes to become a coin designer? The current team includes artists who illustrate books and design toys, dolls, and action figures. Now that's a creative crew!

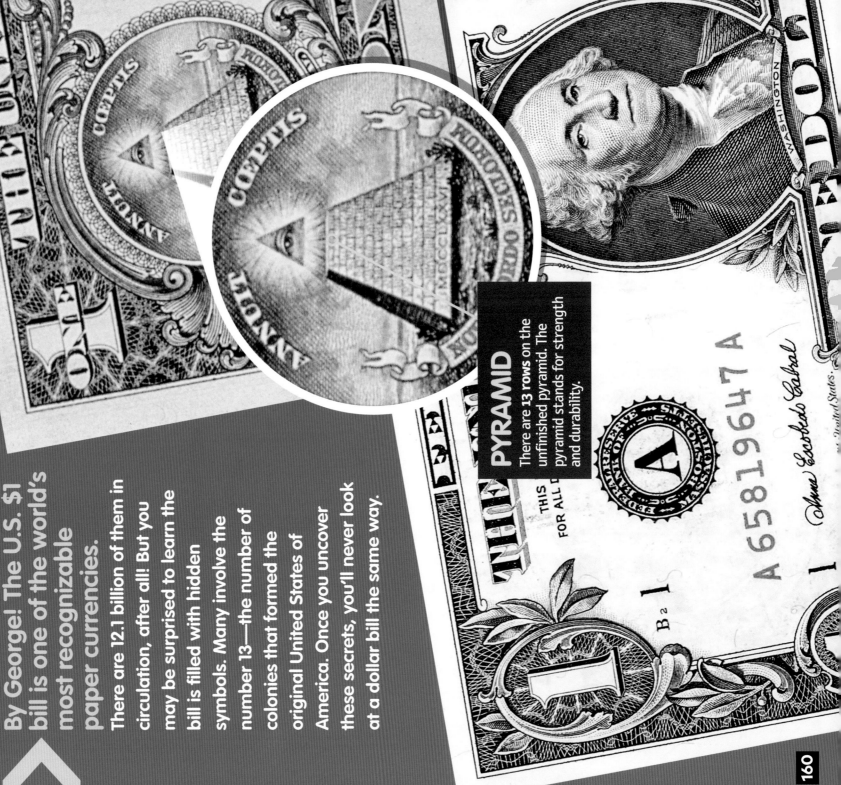

HIDDEN
on a one-dollar bill

By George! The U.S. $1 bill is one of the world's most recognizable paper currencies.

There are 12.1 billion of them in circulation, after all! But you may be surprised to learn the bill is filled with hidden symbols. Many involve the number 13—the number of colonies that formed the original United States of America. Once you uncover these secrets, you'll never look at a dollar bill the same way.

PYRAMID

There are **13 rows** on the unfinished pyramid. The pyramid stands for strength and durability.

EAGLE'S SHIELD

The shield on the eagle's chest contains two important parts. There is a horizontal bar, representing Congress, the body of government that makes laws for the nation. And there are **13 stripes** of alternating green and white supporting the bar that represent the original colonies.

LEAVES AND OLIVES

The eagle's right leg grips an olive branch bearing **13 leaves** and **13 olives**. The olive branch represents peace. The eagle is facing the right side to emphasize the power of peace over war.

ARROWS

Clutched in the talons of the eagle's left foot are **13 arrows.** The arrows signify the country's readiness to fight.

FRONT SIDE

The seal of the U.S. Treasury Department is pictured on the front of the bill. In the center of the seal are **13 stars.** This seal has been printed on nearly all U.S. paper currency since 1862.

STARS

Above the eagle's head is a constellation of **13 stars.** The constellation symbolizes the formation of a new nation.

People toss about

$1.5 MILLION

in coins into the Trevi! Fountain

in Rome, Italy, each year.

WHERE DOES ALL THAT MONEY GO?

According to legend, if you toss a coin over your shoulder into Rome's Trevi Fountain, you'll return to the city one day. A second coin is said to bring love, and a third, marriage. (There's even an old song about it called "Three Coins in the Fountain.") How many Trevi wishes actually come true will forever be a mystery, but what happens to all that cold, wet cash isn't mysterious at all. A few mornings a week, Roman police officers stand guard as workers rake the coins into long rows and then use an underwater vacuum to suck up the jingling piles. Volunteers get out the soap and clean the coins, and then count them up. The money goes to a good cause—helping homeless and hungry people in Rome. That's a wish everyone can get behind!

EPIC EXTREMES

Biggest, rainiest, most expensive—our big, wide world is filled with remarkable record breakers and extraordinary extremes. There's a tree that weighs more than 100 elephants, a place where it rains nearly 500 inches (1,270 cm) a year, a pizza with actual gold on it, and a 750-leg creepy crawler. These might seem too extreme to be true, but they are the real deal. Read on to explore the most extreme things on our planet, and encounter people whose fantastic feats are truly epic.

COOL CROCS

They have long, knifelike teeth, skin like armor, huge yellow eyes with slit pupils, and the patience of an ambush hunter.

Crocodiles are among the most fearsome yet amazing creatures on Earth. Uncover some of their most incredible secrets.

COLOSSAL CROC

Male saltwater crocodiles average 16 feet (5 m) in length—about half as long as a school bus. The largest saltie ever recorded was a male measuring just over 20 feet (6 m). Females are much smaller, about half the size of males.

BIGGEST BITE

The saltwater crocodile has the most powerful jaws in the animal kingdom. This champion chomper has a bite force of 3,700 pounds per square inch (260 kg/sq cm)—nearly 25 times that of a human. Scientists think a 20-foot (6-m) saltie might come close to the bite power of *Tyrannosaurus rex*, which had the strongest known bite of any dinosaur. A saltie's teeth can be up to five inches (13 cm) long—that's about the height of a soda can!

GO WITH THE FLOW

All crocs spend a lot of time in water, but salties are unique—they travel distances as far as 30 miles (48 km) or more down rivers and out to sea. You'd think they'd be great swimmers, but they actually surf the currents more than they swim. Just as important as their ability to surf: their patience. When they want to travel in the ocean, they wait for exactly the right conditions and then hitch a ride on a fast-moving ocean current. When the tide turns in the wrong direction, these crocs haul out onto land, such as an island, to wait for favorable conditions to return.

BABY ON BOARD

Crocodile mothers carry their newly hatched babies to the water in their mouth. They can carry up to 15 little crocs at one time.

BACKUP TEETH

Most crocs have more than 60 super-sharp teeth. The smallest, the dwarf crocodile, has about 30 teeth. Like sharks, crocodiles have replacement teeth at the ready. Whenever they lose a tooth, a new one soon takes its place. A croc can go through thousands of teeth in a lifetime.

SWAMP BUFFET

Crocs are classic ambush hunters. They lurk just beneath the water's surface, waiting for prey looking to take a drink at the water's edge. Then they pounce! Favorite dishes include water buffalo, birds, and fish—and for saltwater crocs, even sharks that swim close to shore. Gharials, a croc relative, have a different hunting habit. They can sense movement in the water through special cells in their snouts that act like motion detectors. By swinging their snouts back and forth in the water, gharials find fish to feed on.

Rock climber Alex Honnold took only

FOUR HOURS TO CLIMB

a 3,000-foot (914-m) rock face—
without using any ropes
or safety gear.

HOW DID THIS COURAGEOUS CLIMBER DO IT?

It was a feat most rock climbers thought was impossible. Alex Honnold scaled the face of Yosemite National Park's El Capitan, U.S.A., without using ropes or safety equipment, a climbing method called free soloing. Even with gear, this famous cliff in California is extremely challenging. Some sections of granite rock wall are smooth vertical slabs with no cracks or crevices to cling to.

"It's like walking up glass," said Honnold. His achievement is considered the most daring and dangerous free solo accomplishment ever. The key to his success? According to Honnold, it was his ability to remain calm during the climb.

The astounding ascent took less than four hours to complete, but it required more than a year of planning. "You have to prepare to the point where it's just not scary at all," Honnold said. He studied the route, precisely mapped out each movement—where he would place his hands and feet as he climbed—and practiced each segment over and over until he felt comfortable doing it without ropes. A particularly perilous part known as the Freeblast required more than 90 practice runs. For this pro climber, practice really did make perfect.

The cliff, called El Capitan, is higher than the world's tallest building, Burj Khalifa.

The oldest giant sequoia has been standing for more than 3,500 years. It was alive during the days of King Tut.

Researchers climb to towering heights to study sequoias.

SECRETS of GIANT

These towering trees are superheroes of the forest: They're super tall—the largest trees on Earth; they're super old—living 3,000 years or more; and they're super strong—once they mature, they're practically indestructible. Meet the giant sequoias, and prepare to discover the secrets to their super survival.

Land of Thirsty Giants

California is the only place in the world where giant sequoias are found. They require an enormous amount of water to thrive: up to 800 gallons (3,028 L) per day! The sweet spot for these trees is elevations between 5,000 and 7,000 feet (1,524 and 2,134 m). At lower altitudes the soil is too dry; higher up, temperatures are too cold. The western slopes of California's Sierra Nevada mountains are perfect for these thirsty world wonders. Here, in this so-called Land of Giants, snow accumulates over the winter months and soaks into the ground in summer, resulting in wonderfully wet soil.

Supersize Tree!

Giant sequoias may not be the world's tallest trees (that honor goes to the coastal redwood), but they are the largest measured by volume. The biggest of them all, nicknamed General Sherman, is the most massive living tree in the world. Weighing in at four million pounds (1.8 million kg), this towering titan weighs the same as 13 blue whales, or 107 elephants, or 2,500 polar bears!

Just its trunk measures 52,500 cubic feet (1,487 cu m)—equal to the amount of cement in 194 cement mixers.

The sequoia's extraordinary size is linked to its long life span. While humans stop growing by the time they reach adulthood, sequoias continue to grow throughout their lives. In fact, they grow *faster* as they age. That's because older trees have wider crowns (the foliage and tree branches), which contain more leaves, allowing them to generate more energy through photosynthesis (the process all trees use to turn sunlight into food).

Plant-astic Plumbing

You might expect trees this tall to have very deep roots, but actually, sequoia roots rarely grow more than three feet

SEQUOIAS

(1 m) below ground. Instead of down, they spread out far and wide—sometimes extending more than 150 feet (46 m) away from the base of the trunk. The huge amount of water that giant sequoias need has to be transported up from these roots to the tops of the trees, all while traveling against the force of gravity.

Sequoias have ingenious internal plumbing. Tubelike structures within the trees act as pipelines, carrying water from the roots to the tops of the trees through narrow tubes called xylem. Other wider tubes called phloem carry nutrients back down. While all trees need a system like this to move water, giant conifers (evergreen trees) such as sequoias have narrower tubes than hardwoods like oak or maple.

The tube systems work like a straw. A narrow straw requires less sucking pressure to pull up liquid from a cup. So it's similar to how you only need to take a small sip to drink from a narrow little juice box straw, versus the harder pull you need to take on a wide bubble tea or milkshake straw. The narrow tubes of the sequoias make it easier for water to travel to the tops of these living skyscrapers, which means they can keep growing and growing.

Only the Tough Survive

Being big isn't all that matters. Their toughness is also legendary. Most sequoias can survive situations in which many other trees wouldn't stand a chance, such as wildfires, fungi, and wood-munching bugs. And it's all thanks

to the sequoia's bark. It's famous for its dark red color, caused by chemicals called tannins. Tannins are a natural defense against fungi, which love moist environments like California forests. The bark is also three feet (1 m) thick, which helps shield the tree from burrowing bugs. It acts as a kind of firewall, too, protecting the tree from flames. While fire can damage the trees, it seldom kills adult ones. A sequoia can even survive being hollowed out by fire. The Chimney Tree at Sequoia National Park has a burned-out interior, but its outer shell continues to grow.

With all these secret powers, it's no wonder sequoias are survival superstars!

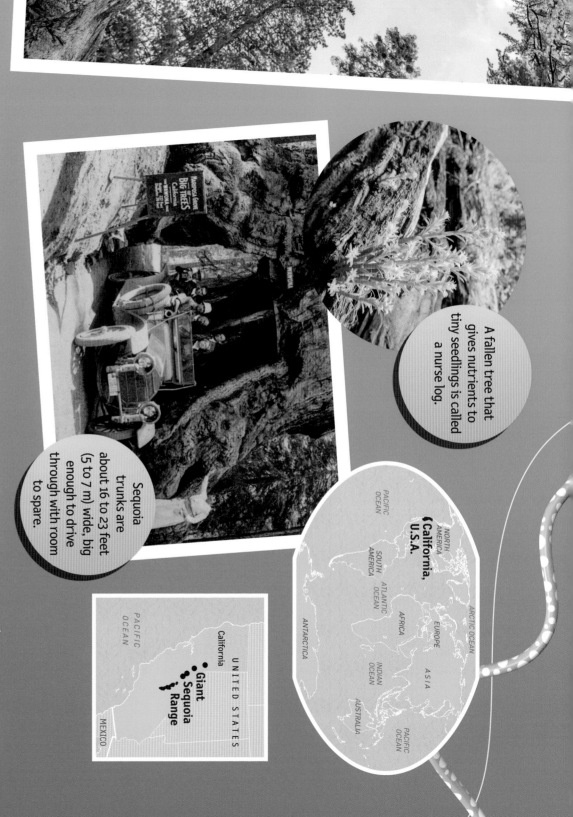

A fallen tree that gives nutrients to tiny seedlings is called a nurse log.

Sequoia trunks are about 16 to 23 feet (5 to 7 m) wide, big enough to drive through with room to spare.

California, U.S.A.

NORTH AMERICA
SOUTH AMERICA
ANTARCTICA
EUROPE
AFRICA
ASIA
AUSTRALIA
PACIFIC OCEAN
ATLANTIC OCEAN
ARCTIC OCEAN
INDIAN OCEAN
PACIFIC OCEAN

UNITED STATES
California
Giant Sequoia Range
PACIFIC OCEAN
MEXICO

EXTREME ANIMAL RECORDS

THERE'S SOMETHING AMAZING ABOUT SUPERLATIVES. WHO'S THE BIGGEST AND BOLDEST, THE FASTEST AND MOST FLATULENT? ESPECIALLY WHEN IT COMES TO ANIMALS, WE WANT TO KNOW! READ ON TO UNLOCK THE RECORD-BREAKING TALENTS OF FIVE EXTREME ANIMALS.

SPEEDY SPRINTER

With lean muscles, powerful hind legs, and a long, flexible spine, this cat was born to run. A cheetah named Sarah at the Cincinnati Zoo in the U.S. completed a 100-meter dash in just 5.95 seconds, making her the fastest land animal. How do humans stack up? Olympian Usain Bolt ran the same distance in 9.58 seconds.

PUTRID PROTECTION

It has zebralike stripes and a foul-smelling spray like a skunk, but the striped polecat, also called a zorilla, stands apart from other animals. It's one of the smelliest around! Fifteen different chemicals combine to make the striper's spray remarkably repulsive. Its super-foul odor is so bad that, according to one report, the stench was strong enough to protect a single striped polecat from a pride of hungry lions.

ENORMOUS EGG-STRAVAGANZA

It may look like a giant swimming pancake, but this fish is no stranger to being large and in charge. The ocean sunfish, or mola, is the largest bony fish beneath the waves, weighing up to 2.5 tons (2.3 t). But while these massive marine animals may be big, their eggs are teeny tiny. Each of the 300 million eggs they release is .05 inches (.13 cm) across—so small that about 27 would fit on a single sesame seed.

SEA SIGHT

These shellfish have their eyes on the prize—all 200 of them! A scallop may look like just a beautiful shell, but inside there's a brilliant bivalve with superpowerful peepers. A poppy seed–size eye sits on the tip of each tentacle, visible when the animal opens its shell. Each eye has a mini-mirror that reflects images onto two retinas. One retina focuses on what's in front of the eye, while the other takes in the scallop's surroundings. Scientists think there's a lot more to these amazing organs than meets the eye. They not only allow the shellfish to see predators underwater, but the way a scallop's eyes work is similar to technology used today in deep-space telescopes. In the future, researchers hope to study scallops to build better underwater cameras.

BIG BABY

A blue whale starts life as one of the planet's biggest creatures. At birth, it weighs up to 6,000 pounds (2,721 kg) and is 23 feet (7 m) long—longer than a pickup truck. Then it grows bigger, and bigger, and bigger, packing on about 200 pounds (91 kg) a day during its first year of life. This massive growth spurt is powered by milk. A blue whale mother's milk is exceptionally high in fat, and her baby drinks a lot of it—up to 50 gallons (190 L) in a single day.

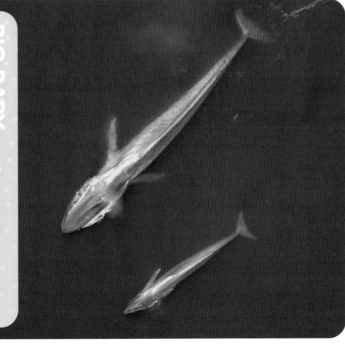

EXTREME EATS

EAT TO LIVE OR LIVE TO EAT? There's some of each in the world of extreme food. These tales of gastronomic adventure are sure to make you hungry for more.

PRIZE-WINNING STOMACHS

The world's most famous hot dog–eating contest is held each year on the Fourth of July at Coney Island in New York City. Contestants compete to see who can eat the most frankfurters in 10 minutes. Joey Chestnut has taken the top prize 12 times. He holds the record with a stomach-turning 74! Competitive eaters train for events by doing practice runs with days of rest between. Pro eating events are so popular that there's even a world governing organization that sets rules, and ranks eaters. There is an eating contest for just about everything, from tacos and pizza to oysters and spicy kimchi.

HOLD THE PEPPERONI

For the same price, you could buy 180 large pizzas from your local pizzeria, or you could order a single 24K pizza from one New York City eatery. At $2,700, it's the most expensive pizza in the world. This pricey pie can't be a last-minute lunch decision; due to its exceptional ingredients, it must be ordered 48 hours in advance. The special squid-ink dough must rest for two days before being stretched. Other top-shelf ingredients include Stilton cheese flown in from Britain, truffles from France, and caviar from the Caspian Sea. And to top it off—edible 24-karat gold leaf. That's one expensive slice!

CANNED CUISINE

For many people, canned ham like Spam is the ultimate survival food. It is long-lasting, and opens with a pull-top, making it handy in an emergency. But for Hawaiians, canned ham is more than that. It's a daily food staple, served with everything from sushi to sorbet. More canned ham is sold in Hawaii—nearly seven million cans each year—than in any other U.S. state. The state celebrates this obsession by hosting the annual Spam Jam, a hugely popular food festival that attracts thousands of visitors from around the globe.

SWEET LIBERTY

Husband and wife sculptors Jim Victor and Marie Pelton have a real appetite for extreme masterpieces. They carved a likeness of the U.S. Capitol building out of a 400-pound (181-kg) block of cheddar—enough cheese to make more than 5,000 sandwiches! They've sculpted another Washington landmark—the White House—out of butter, and their 800-pound (363-kg) chocolate replica of the Statue of Liberty is on display in a Las Vegas hotel. That's some appetizing architecture!

HANDLE WITH CARE

Surströmming may be tasty, but this fish dish is considered by many to have the foulest fumes of any food on the planet. The smell is so bad that airlines have banned it from flights! Surströmming, also called sour herring, is made by salting the fish and fermenting it—first in barrels, then sealed in cans. A "surströmming premiere" in August marks the date when the fish is fully fermented and ready to eat. People go to great lengths to avoid the stench and spurting juices when opening the cans. Some open them underwater, and gloves are a must. A Swedish custom for more than 500 years, sour herring is traditionally eaten in a sandwich.

SECRETS of WILD WAVES

Dolphins love to ride waves; experts think they may do it to conserve energy, communicate, find mates, or just have fun!

n 1826, a French naval officer described seeing ocean waves topping 100 feet (30 m) high. People said his claim was ridiculous. Impossible, even! At the time, most scientists thought waves could not be higher than 30 feet (9 m).

For more than a century, reports of monster waves were dismissed as myth, no more believable than tales of mermaids and sea dragons. Today, we know they are a real phenomenon. What causes these wild waves and sets them apart from the ones we see at the beach is more than just a tall tale.

Waves and Wind

From gentle ripples to towering walls of water, the ocean's waves take many forms. But the force that makes all waves, big and small, is energy. Winds blow across the ocean and pull and push on its surface. This transfer of energy sets the water in motion.

A wave's size depends on several factors, including the speed of the wind and the distance the wind travels. The largest waves occur where winds travel great distances across the ocean, building up lots of energy along the way.

Wall of Water

A tsunami is a massive wave or set of waves caused by a sudden disturbance to the seafloor, such as an earthquake or a volcanic eruption. The disturbance creates a force of energy that pushes water up, creating a series of waves that surge onto shore.

Out at sea, tsunamis are barely visible. But since the water is shallower at the coastline, the waves build to towering heights by the time they hit land. Sometimes, before a tsunami hits, there is a huge vacuum effect, and water is sucked away from beaches. Minutes later, the first giant wave strikes the shore. In earthquake-prone areas such as Hawaii and Japan, warning signals let people know when a tsunami is coming.

Tsunamis carry debris into the ocean that can turn up later on remote coasts. On April 7, 2013, a small, battered boat washed ashore in Crescent City, California. Japanese characters on the boat's hull helped solve the mystery of where it had come from. The vessel belonged to a high school in Rikuzentakata, a Japanese village 4,750 miles (7,644 km) away. Two years earlier, an earthquake in Japan had triggered a tsunami, which swept the boat out to sea. Students in Crescent

City repaired the boat and raised money to send it back to Japan. The little boat not only survived the incredible voyage but also launched friendships that stretched across the ocean.

The Wildest of Waves

Waves moving through the ocean travel at different speeds and in different directions. If they intersect under the right conditions, they reinforce one another, turning into a single monumental wave known as a rogue wave. While rogue waves are large, there isn't a particular size that defines them. To be considered rogue, a wave must be at least twice the height of the big waves in the area where they occur. Utterly unpredictable, rogues rise suddenly from the sea.

The first one ever scientifically

recorded was an 84-footer (25.6-m) that occurred off the coast of Norway in 1995. That event cast previous sightings—such as the one reported by that 19th-century French captain—in a new light. Since then, even larger rogues have been measured, including a 91-foot (28-m) wave in the Gulf of Mexico in 2004 during Hurricane Ivan. Scientists estimate that ocean motion goes rogue once every 10,000 waves. As the planet's climate warms, experts predict rogues will become more common, because warmer oceans mean more storms and more energy pushing all that water around.

Understanding the what, why, and where of waves helps us make plans for future wild wave events.

Wintertime storms in the North Atlantic Ocean push huge waves toward Europe, pounding coastlines, like this one in Porto, Portugal.

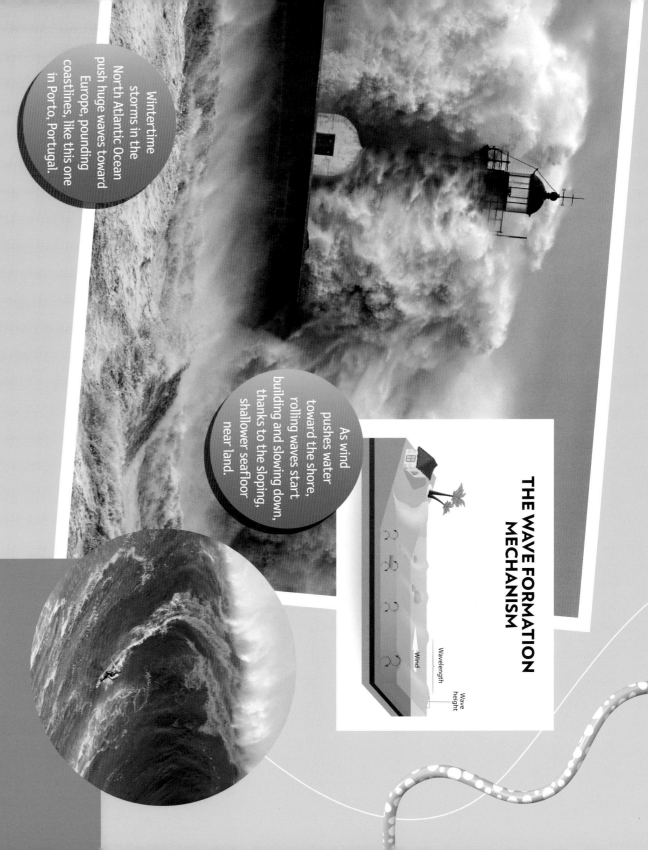

THE WAVE FORMATION MECHANISM

As wind pushes water toward the shore, rolling waves start building and slowing down, thanks to the sloping, shallower seafloor near land.

Wind

Wavelength

Wave height

SURF'S UP— WAY UP

The seaside town of Nazaré, Portugal, is famous for its epic waves. As much as 10 stories high, these waves form because of a deep canyon right off the coast. Water squeezes into the canyon's cliffs and ledges and is pushed up by the force of the relentless flow. This creates unusually large waves. Wherever there are big breakers, there are thrill-seeking big-wave surfers. To qualify as "big" in the extreme sport of big-wave surfing, a wave must be at least 20 feet (6 m) high. The biggest ever surfed, in November 2017, was an 80-foot (24-m) wave in Nazaré. Talk about making a splash!

ASK AN EXPERT

Underwater drones assist with aquaculture—farming shellfish in the ocean—by spotting signs of predators or algae that can damage oysters.

How do scientists use **robots** to explore the extreme depths of the **ocean?**

THE EXPERT: Erika Bergman, National Geographic Explorer, submarine pilot, founder of the Girls Underwater Robot Camps

Q WHAT'S THE MOST SPECTACULAR OCEAN TO EXPLORE?

A: Rather than a geographic location, it's a depth. There's a layer in the ocean called the mesopelagic, or the twilight zone. It ranges from about 650 to 3,300 feet (200 to 1,000 m) deep, depending on where you are in the ocean. The greatest migration on the planet takes place in the mesopelagic layer, and it happens every single day. It's this huge migration of microscopic plankton that are followed by bigger fish and then even bigger fish, until you have all these predators chasing smaller prey. To explore the mesopelagic layer, you need a submarine, of course.

Masses of plankton migrate for survival: to get a meal in the upper layers where plants grow in sunlight and to avoid predators in the lower, mesopelagic layer.

Q WHEN ARE ROVS (REMOTE-OPERATED VEHICLES) USED TO EXPLORE THE OCEAN'S DEPTHS?

A: We use submarines strictly for observation. ROVs are better at doing work underwater. They can carry big manipulator arms and other equipment, and can be used to conduct long transects (underwater surveys). An ROV can be underwater for a month, whereas a piloted submersible can only stay underwater for a few hours.

Q DO YOU HAVE TO BE AN EXPERT TO OPERATE AN ROV?

A: One type of ROV that's very accessible, even to young people, is called the OpenROV. It's a little underwater robot that you can drive using a cell phone. It lets you explore 300 feet (90 m) below the surface, which is so much deeper than people can swim. Anyone can build one of these OpenROVs with some basic electronic components and simple programming.

Q WHAT IS IT LIKE TO PILOT A SUBMARINE?

A: It only takes a few minutes to learn how to fly the submarine, but it takes a lifetime to master the different conditions that the ocean might throw at you. Now, after 10 years of flying submarines, I feel like I have a good handle on a lot of parts of the ocean, and I have a lot of experience underwater. But if you have a trained pilot in the submarine who hands you the controller, anybody can drive it around. It's easy! The controller is like a video game joystick. But managing life support, operating sonar equipment, dealing with emergency situations, and keeping calm under pressure—these things take longer to master.

Q WHAT ADVICE DO YOU HAVE FOR FUTURE EXPLORERS?

A: You're never too young to start. If you close your eyes and think of something you want to explore, and how you're going to do it—really focus on the how—I almost guarantee you're going to come up with an idea that only you have ever thought of. Which means you're the only person in the entire world who can lead that expedition. So you'd better do it, because nobody else is going to!

Millipedes can have up to 750 LEGS,

making them

MEET THE ANIMAL THAT'S ALWAYS A STEP AHEAD

While people often think millipedes have 1,000 legs (the word means "thousand feet," after all), most actually have fewer than 400. Some standout species have hundreds more, though: One found in California can have up to 750 little legs, and wins the award for the leggiest creature.

Having hundreds of pairs of legs would slow most critters down. But this animal's appendages weren't made for walking. Instead, millipedes use them to tunnel through the ground, so they can eat their way through decaying plants and fungi, which in turn helps make the soil healthy. They also use their burrowing power to hide from predators, such as ants, beetles, birds, and badgers. If hiding doesn't work, many millipedes take extreme steps, with chemicals that they unload from their defensive glands. Some species secrete chemicals that just taste terrible, while others produce deadlier concoctions. Yellow-spotted millipedes protect themselves with cyanide, in doses that wouldn't injure a person but can be fatal to small mammals and birds. That's one way to stand up for yourself!

the leggiest animals on Earth.

Some also produce
deadly chemicals in amounts
powerful enough to
kill 18 birds!

That's SUPER
COOL!

RECORD-BREAKING ADVENTURES

TOO HOT TO HANDLE

The Lut Desert in southeast Iran is so hot that scientists once thought it was impossible for animals or plants to live there. A NASA satellite logged a ground temperature of 159.3°F (70.7°C) in 2005, and it's still the highest ever recorded anywhere on Earth. Lut is famous for its amazing windswept dunes, but its landscape also includes salt plains, giant rock formations, sinkholes, and ravines—making it look like a planet straight out of science fiction. The desert is uninhabitable for people, but foxes, reptiles, insects, and spiders all make this scorching spot their home.

SOGGY STAY

Mawsynram, a village in India, was declared the world's wettest place after receiving 1,000 inches (2,540 cm) of rain in one year. That would fill tens of thousands of Olympic-size swimming pools. Its annual average is 467 inches (1,186 cm)—more than 12 times that of Seattle, a U.S. city with a reputation for rain. During the peak monsoon months of June and July, when heavy rains combine with high winds, there are daily downpours in Mawsynram. People who work outside wear *knups*—hands-free umbrellas made from bamboo frames covered with woven banana leaves—to stay dry.

SALTY SPA DAY

It sounds strange, but in the special lake known as the Dead Sea, you can float without a raft. The extremely salty water makes things super buoyant. The Dead Sea is extreme in many ways: It's the saltiest body of water on the planet (saltier than the ocean or the Great Salt Lake in Utah, U.S.A.). This body of water is also the lowest point on Earth at 1,365 feet (416 m) below sea level. The climate here is hot and dry: daytime temperatures range from 70°F (21°C) in winter to 100°F (38°C) in summer, and it rains only about two inches (5 cm) a year. Oh, and about that name: Nothing can live in the Dead Sea because of its high mineral content. These minerals, though, are great for the skin!

DRY AS DUST

A little rain isn't newsworthy in most places. But when it sprinkled in the center of Chile's Atacama Desert in 2015, it was the first measurable precipitation in the spot in 500 years. Its location between mountain ranges, plus environmental factors, keep the rain away. Scientists believe some areas of this desert have never seen rain at all, and there are riverbeds that have been dry for more than 100,000 years.

CHILLY CITY

Furry hats and icy eyelashes are a common sight in Yakutsk, Russia, the coldest city on Earth. For four months of the year, temperatures in this Siberian spot never reach above 0°F (-18°C). And the digits can dip further: The lowest ever recorded was -83°F (-64°C). But Yakutsk has another claim to fame: It's home to the world's only museum dedicated to the woolly mammoth, with Ice Age fossils that are more than 14,000 years old.

HIGHEST SPOT

To get as close to space as possible by foot, climb to the peak of Mount Chimborazo, an inactive volcano in the South American country of Ecuador. There, you'll be standing at the farthest point from the center of Earth—even farther than the summit of Mount Everest. Our planet bulges at the middle, giving mountain ranges like Chimborazo along the Equator a big boost toward the outer limits.

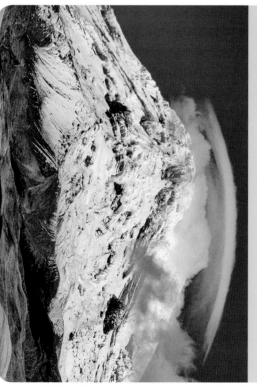

According to some stories, when the kraken descended into the deep, it caused a powerful whirlpool that sucked in everything above it.

Some experts think there may be more than one species of giant squid.

QUEST FOR THE KRAKEN

As far back as the 12th century, tales of huge, tentacled sea monsters have thrilled, chilled, and terrified humans. Norwegian seafarers dubbed these awesome beasts "kraken." By the 19th century, the kraken still had a fearsome reputation. The sea monster's legendarily long, suction cup–covered tentacles could reach the top of a ship's main mast. It was known to dig its sharp, curved claws into boats, stare sailors in the face with its dinner plate–size eyeballs, and then drag them to the bottom of the sea without a second thought. This is one seriously scary sea monster. But is it real?

MONSTERS OF THE DEEP

There are real, live giant squid in our oceans. These spectacular cephalopods were first described by a Danish naturalist in 1857 and have made rare (but memorable) appearances since. In 2004, Japanese scientists reeled one onto their research vessel.

When scientists hauled the appendage into the boat, they were startled to see it still wriggling! The 18-foot (5.5-m) tentacle slithered across the deck, then latched onto a scientist's arm with teeth-lined suckers. Could this be the legendary kraken?

STUDYING SQUID

Scientists suspect the giant squid is the inspiration for the kraken legend. As big as a school bus, this titan prowls the lightless depths of the ocean preying on other squid and even whales. But scientists don't know much about them, since they are difficult to study. Giant squid live about 6,560 feet (2,000 m) below the surface of Antarctic waters. For decades, researchers only knew the species existed from carcasses that washed up on beaches. The Japanese scientists who tussled with the creature in 2004 reeled in a living specimen two years later. They said the 24-foot (7-m) beast put up quite a fight as they hauled it aboard. And it was only a baby!

The creature tussled with the crew and finally broke free, severing one of its tentacles in the battle.

DEEP-SEA MYSTERY

From studying the bodies of giant squid that wash up on shore, experts think they weigh about half a ton (453 kg) each. The longest ever found measured 59 feet (18 m). That's big—but it's not as big as the kraken described by sailors. Could a colossal squid be masquerading as the crazy kraken? Without more evidence and eyewitness accounts, we might never get to the depths of this mystery.

The largest giant squid ever found is more than half the size of the largest animal on the planet!

Giant Squid 59 feet (19 m)

Blue Whale up to 105 feet (32 m)

CREDITS

Abbreviations: AG = Age Fotostock; AS = Alamy Stock Photo; DS = Dreamstime; GI = Getty Images; IS = iStock; NG = National Geographic Image Collection; SS = Shutterstock

Cover (astronaut), capitanoseye/SS; (spider), Debbie Hall/Caters News; mountainpix/SS; (volcano), Olivier Grunewald; (roller coaster), Six Flags/Splash News/Newscom; (lizard), Ken Griffiths/IS; spine (lizard), Ken Griffiths/IS; back (dog), Nat NT/GI; (sand dune), Melissa Cherry Villumsen/iliveasidream.com; (skateboarder), Sean M. Haffey/GI

Chapter 1: 6, Heeb Christian/AG; 8-9, Jozev/IS; 10 (UP), Giuglio Gil/AG; 10 (LO), santirf/IS; 11 (UP), Stephen J Boitano/GI; 11 (CTR), Edmund Sumner/AG; 11 (LO), AP Images/Chen jun - Imaginechina; 12-13, Six Flags/Splash News/Newscom; 14, Funkystock/AG; 14-15, OlegAlbinsky/IS; 15, Buurserstraat386/DS; 16, T Photography/SS 16-17, Dave Stamboulis/AG; 17 (UP), holgs/IS; 17 (LO LE), tatyun/IS; 17 (LO RT), DavidStorm/IS; 18-19, kenneth geiger/NG; 19 (LO CTR), Takranik/IS; 19 (LO RT), Jason Hawkes/GI; 20 (UP LE), dreamikon/SS; 20 (UP RT), Piti Sirisriro/DS; 20 (LO LE), Jody Ann/SS; 20 (LO RT), Vadim_An/IS; 21 (UP LE), sumikophoto/SS; 21 (UP RT), David_Bodescu/ISphoto; 23, CSP_Media/AG; 24-25, Jason Treat, NGP Staff/Skidmore, Owings & Merrill (SOM)/National Geographic Partners

Chapter 2: 26-27, cgteam/AG; 28 (UP), Michael Krabs/imageBROKER/AG; 28 (LO), stock_photo_world/SS; 29 (UP LE), Rpianoshow/DS; 29 (UP RT), Luis Javier Sandoval/VW Pics/StockTrek Images; 29 (LO LE), The India Today Group/GI; 29 (LO RT), Ehrlif/DS; 30-31, Stephen Dalton/Minden Pictures/AG; 32, Rebecca Yale/GI; 33 (UP LE), Ethan Daniels/SS; 33 (UP RT), Dr. Antonio Machado; 33 (LO), Carles Soler/AG; 34-35, AmericanWildlife/AG; 36, 3DSculptor/IS; 37 (UP), Marc Ward/StockTrek Images; 37 (LO), NASA; 38 (UP), Tools of Marketing, Inc.; 38 (LO), Chun Kit Ho/DS; 39 (LE), Sudong Kim/SS; 39 (RT), VC-DLH/Prisma/AG; 40, DEA/G Dagli Orti/AG; 40-41, Bjorn Landstrom/NG; 41, Victor R. Boswell Jr./NG; 42 (UP), Jarno Gonzalez Zarraonandia/SS; 42 (LO), Photodisc; 43 (UP), Simon Fletcher/DS; 43 (CTR), SuperStock/AG; 43 (LO), Michael Runkel/imageBROKER/AG; 44, metamorworks/IS; GI; 44-45, AR infotainment interface for self-driving cars by WayRay

Chapter 3: 46, Armoo1/AG; 48-49, Nat NT/GI; 50 (UP), Steve Downer/ardea/AG; 50 (LO), Ken Griffiths/IS; 51 (UP LE), Amazon-Images/AS; 51 (UP RT), David Havel/DS; 51 (LO), Lee Amery/DS; 52, Richard Robinson/AG; 53 (UP RT), Chris Brunskill/ardea.com/AG; 53 (LO LE), Phil Motta at the University of South Florida; 53 (LO RT), Alan Dawson/AG; 54, S. Gerth/AG; 55 (UP), FLPA/Roger Tidman/AG; 55 (LO), Mitsuaki Iwago/AG; 56, Michael S. Nolan/AG; 56-57, Michael Gore/FLPA/AG; 57 (LE), Tom Soucek/AG; 57 (RT), ROBERT67/SS; 58-59, Simon Fletcher/DS; 59, Fernando G. Baptista/NG; 60-61, Flip Nicklin/Minden Pictures; 62 (UP LE), Conservationist/SS; 62 (LO), Satoshi Kuribayashi/Minden Pictures; 63 (UP LE), Kelvin Aitken/WWPics/AG; 63 (UP RT), Joan Egert/DS; 63 (LO), Fernando Romão/AS; 64), Jim Cumming/SS; 65 (UP LE), Jocrebbin/DS; 65 (UP RT), Feathercollector/DS; 65 (CTR RT), Melinda Fawver/SS; 65 (CTR LE), KeithSzafranski/IS; 66 (LO), Matthijs Kuijpers/DS; 67 (UP), Ben Mcleish/DS; 67 (CTR LE), Anna Podekova/DS; 67 (CTR RT), reptiles4all/SS; 67 (LO), Picstudio/DS

Chapter 4: 68-69, Franco Tempesta; 70-71, SuperStock/AG; 72, Jose Fuste Raga/AG; 72-73, Dmitry Rukhlenko/DS; 73 (UP), Happystock/Dreamstme; 73 (LO), The Proceedings of the National Academy of Sciences (PNAS); 74, wundervisuals/IS; 75 (UP), fototeca gilardi/AG; 75 (LO), DarioEgidi/IS; 76, Last Refuge/AG; 76-77, David Herraez/DS; 77 (UP), SeanPavonePhoto/AG; 77 (LO), WitR/ISphoto; 78-79, Sam Kennedy; 80 (UP), Franco Tempesta; 80 (LO), PlanetFelicity/DS; 81 (UP), Franco Tempesta; 81 (LO), Aunt_Spray/IS; 82 (UP), Mary Evans/Greenville Collins Postcard Collection/AG; 82 (LO), Tim Mannakee/Sime/eStock Photo; 83 (UP), Fletcher Fund, 1935; 83 (CTR LE), Historical Views/AG; 83 (CTR RT), World History Archive/AG; 83 (LO), Museum of London/AG; 84-85, minddream/SS; 86-87 (RT), Vaclav/DS; 87, Roger Ressmeyer/Corbis/VCG/GI

Chapter 5: 88, Albert Russ/SS; 90-91, Yuri Arcurs/agefotostock; 92 (UP), Hannah Mckay/Reuters/Newscom; 92 (LO), Martin Acosta/picture-alliance/dpa/Newscom; 93 (UP), CDC/James Archer; 93 (CTR LE), The Park Spark Project courtesy of artist

Matthew Mazzotta; 93 (CTR RT), Adek Berry/Stringer/GI; 93 (LO), Francisco Kjolseth/The Salt Lake Tribune; 94, Lockheed Martin/NASA; 95 (UP LE), Photos courtesy of Kevin Ma and Pakpong Chirarattananon, Harvard John A. Paulson School of Engineering and Applied Sciences; 95 (UP RT), Nymi Inc; 95 (LO), Paul Zinken/dpa/agefotostock; 96-97, Bryan Brazil/SS; 97, Cody Duncan/agefotostock; 98-99, Justin Hofman/NG; 99, AE Pictures Inc/Photodisc/GI; 100, The Crystal Caves in Atherton, Queensland, Australia; 101 (UP), Epitavi/CanStock Photo; 101 (LO), Breck P. Kent/SS; 102-103, Brian Bevan/ardea/AG; 104, melis/AG; 104-105, Judy Darby/DS; 105, Austrophoto/AG

Chapter 6: 106, Kelpfish/DS; 108-109, Melissa Cherry Villumsen/iliveasidream.com; 110, Thitisak Mongkonnimpat/GI; 111 (UP), Olivier Grunewald; 111 (LO), Aliaksandr Mazurkevich/DS; 112 (UP), mr Timmi/SS; 112 (LO), Agil Leonardo/SS; 112-113, jesselindemann/IS; 113 (CTR RT), Yykkaa/DS; 113 (CTR LE), Naum Chayer/AG; 113 (LO), drferry/IS; 114-115, Arhip4/DS; 115 (UP), IgorZh/DS; 115 (LO), Designua/SS; 116 (UP), Most66/DS; 116 (CTR), Jesse Kraft/DS; 116 (LO), Jean-Paul Ferrero/AG; 117 (UP), Michael Scheja/DS; 117 (CTR), Yakthai/DS; 117 (LO), carasava bogdan/SS; 118 (UP), Solvin Zankl/AS; 118 (LO), McPhoto/AG; 118-119 (UP RT), SeaTops/imageBROKER/AG; 118-119 (LO RT), Nature Picture Library/AG; 122, Alaska Stock Images/AG; 123 (UP), Wissanu Sirapat/DS; 123 GFC Collection/AG; 124-125, Freder/GI; 125 (UP), FLPA/Emanuele Biggi/AG; 125 (LO), Daniels/Water/AG; 122, Alaska Stock Images/AG; 119, Stuart Wilson/Science Source; 120-121, Ethan Leonardo Prest Mercon Ro/IS

Chapter 7: 126-127, Cameron Spencer/GI; 128-129, Action Press/Zuma Press; 130, Monica M. Davey/EFE/Newscom: 130-131, UPI/AS: 131, Stokkete/DS; 132 (UP LE), Nationaal Archief/Spaarnestad Photo; 132 (UP RT), IBL Collections/Mary Evans/AG; 132 (LO), World History Archive/AG; 133 (LE), Stephan Jansen/dpa/AG; 133 (RT), Yohei Osada/AG; 134, Richard Maschmeyer/AG; 134-135, I love photo/SS; 135 (UP), Martin Moxter/AG; 135 (LO), Fine Art Images/AG; 136, Cameron Spencer/GI; 136-137, Marcin Kadziolka/SS; 138, Pool/Reuters/Newscom; 139 (UP), Lurii Osadchi/SS; 139 (LO), Borisovv/DS; 140-141, Izf/SS; 142-143, AFLO/AG; 144 (UP LE), Emma Wood/AS; 144 (UP RT), Barry Lewis/AS; 144 (LO LE), Stephanie Pilick/dpa/AG; 144 (LO RT), Ian Melvin/SS; 145 (UP), Claus Schunk/AG; 145 (LO), Pariyawit Sukumpantanasarn/DS

Chapter 8: 146, Fine Art Images/AG; 148 (UP), Kazuhiro Nogi/Staff/GI; 149 (LO LE), Museum of London/AG; 148 (LO RT), NASA; 149 (UP), YM/Color China Photos/Zuma Press; 149 (LO), Historical Views/AG; 150-151, Design Pics/Brian Hillier/Newscom; 152, SuperStock/AG; 153 (UP LE), SuperStock/AG; 153 (UP RT), SuperStock/AG; 153 (LO LE), SuperStock/AG; 153 (LO RT), Fine Art Images/AG; 154, The Forbes Collection; 154-155, Fine Art Images/AG; 155 (UP & LO), The Forbes Collection; 156 (UP), Patrick van Katwijk/Dutch Photo Press/dpa/AG; 156 (LO), CTK Photo/Michal Krumphanzl/AG; 157 (UP), Munsey Fund, 1932; 157 (LO LE), Education Images/UIG/AG; 157 (LO RT), Royal Household Bureau/Xinhua/Alamy Live News; 158, Marijan Murat/imageBROKER/AG; 159 (UP), U.S. Mint; 159 (LO), U.S. Mint; 160-161, Onfokus/IS; 162-163 (UP), Joe Sohm/DS; 162-163 (LO), Brian McEntire

Chapter 9: 164-165, Ian Dyball/SS; 166, Franco Banfi/WaterF/AG; 166-167, AS/AG; 167 (UP LE), Roger De La Harpe/AG; 167 (UP RT), Enrique Ramos López/EyeEm; 167 (LO), Andrea and Antonella Ferrari/AG; 168-169, Jimmy Chin/NG; 170, Anthony Ambrose/UC Berkeley; 170-171, JHVEPhoto/IS; 171 (UP), Andrei Gabriel Stanescu/DS; 171 (LO), Keystone View Company/Library of Congress; 172 (UP), Dick Freder/IS; 172 (LO), Martin Harvey/AG; 173 (UP), Fred Bavendam/AG; 173 (LO LE), Leo Patrizi/IS; 173 (LO RT), Francois Gohier/ardea.com/AG; 174 (UP), Industry Kitchen; 174 (LO), TNYF/WENN.com/AG; 175 (UP LE), Bhofack2/DS; 175 (UP RT), Jeppe Gustafsson/AS; 175 (LO), Lazio Regos Photography/The Hershey Company; 176, AnaDruga/GI/ISphoto; 176-177, Zacarias Pereira da Mata; 177 (UP), Designua/SS; 177 (LO), Gmfiooooi/DS; 178, NG/AS; 179, Andrea Izzotti/SS; 180-181, Danolsen/DS; 182 (LO), Amos Chapple/AG; 183 (UP LE), Philippe Michel/AG; 183 (UP RT), Mehmet0/SS; 182 (UP), Andrea Vetvas/DS; 183 (LO RT), Escudero Patrick/AG; 184-185, Jerry LoFaro/Stockr

End matter: 192, Debbie Hall/Caters News

Some spiders appear in movies (see page 22), and others just look like they do! A tourist spotted this spider, a skeleton look-alike, on a trip to Costa Rica.

Since 1888, the National Geographic Society has funded more than 14,000 research, conservation, education, and storytelling projects around the world. National Geographic Partners distributes a portion of the funds it receives from your purchase to National Geographic Society to support programs including the conservation of animals and their habitats. To learn more, visit natgeo.com/info.

For more information, visit nationalgeographic.com, call 1-877-873-6846, or write to the following address:

National Geographic Partners, LLC
1145 17th Street N.W.
Washington, DC 20036-4688 U.S.A.

For librarians and teachers: nationalgeographic.com/books/librarians-and-educators

More for kids from National Geographic: natgeokids.com

National Geographic Kids magazine inspires children to explore their world with fun yet educational articles on animals, science, nature, and more. Using fresh storytelling and amazing photography, *Nat Geo Kids* shows kids ages 6 to 14 the fascinating truth about the world—and why they should care.
natgeo.com/subscribe

For rights or permissions inquiries, please contact National Geographic Books Subsidiary Rights: bookrights@natgeo.com

Editorial and design by Scout Books and Media Inc.

The publisher would like to thank everyone who made this book possible: From National Geographic: Kate Hale, executive editor; Amanda Larsen, design director; Lori Epstein, director of photography; Joan Gossett, production editorial manager; Vivian Suchman, managing editor; and Gus Tello and Anne LeongSon, design production assistants.

From Scout Books and Media: Susan Knopf, project director; Brenda Scott Royce, author; James Buckley, Jr., contributing writer; Beth Sutinis, editor; Beth Adelman, copyeditor/fact checker; Brittany Schachner, photo research; Andrij Borys, Andrij Borys Associates, designer.

Special thanks also to David Hurst Thomas, Curator, Division of Anthropology, American Museum of Natural History

Hardcover ISBN: 978-1-4263-3858-8
Reinforced library binding ISBN: 978-1-4263-3859-5

Printed in South Korea
23/SPSK/5 (HC)